Dear Parents,

Thank you for purchasing our book. We are thrilled to be part of your child's reading journey. By choosing this book, you have taken an important first step in improving your child's reading skills.

To make the most out of this book, we recommend reading one to two story sets a day for about thirty minutes. Feel free to break this session into two parts if needed to keep your child engaged and focused. After reading and doing the activities, encourage your child to color the picture that accompanies each story. This not only makes learning fun but also reinforces what they have just read.

We understand that starting a new reading program can feel overwhelming, but remember that consistency is key. Setting aside dedicated reading time each day will help build a strong routine and foster a love for reading in your child. If you're unsure where to start, simply start at the beginning and work your way through the book in the order the sets appear. Each short vowel sound has five sets to help your student practice and master the skill.

Additionally, creating a comfortable and distraction-free reading environment can make a significant difference. Choose a quiet spot where your child can concentrate, and make sure they have all the materials they need, including crayons for coloring. Positive reinforcement and praise can also motivate your child and make the learning experience enjoyable.

Should you need any guidance or a FREE placement test, please don't hesitate to reach out. We are here to support you and your child every step of the way. Our goal is to provide you with the tools and resources necessary to make reading a positive and rewarding experience.

Thank you once again for your support. Together, we can make a significant difference in your child's reading journey. Your commitment and involvement play a crucial role in their success, and we are honored to be a part of this important milestone.

Warm regards,
Budding Brains Books

TABLE OF CONTENTS

Blend BL and CL

Blend FL and GL

Blend PL and SL

Blend BR and CR

Blend DR and FR

TABLE OF CONTENTS

Blend GR, TR and PR

Blend SC and SK

Blend SN and SM

Blend SP and ST

Blend SW and TW

TABLE OF CONTENTS

Blend SCR, THR, and SHR

Name: Class:

SET 1
BLEND BL AND CL

Digraph BL, CL Sounds

What's that Sound?

Ask your child to isolate the beginning, middle, or final sound in each word. Alternate each day and adjust the lesson to your student's needs. Do not allow them to see the words or the book while doing this exercise.

Blue	Clad
Bland	Claw
Blur	Club

Blending Sounds

Directions: Ask your child to blend the following sounds into words. Do not show them the page.

Cl-a-w   Bl-u-e

Cl-u-b   Bl-o-b

Cl-a-m   Bl-e-w

Segmenting Sounds

Directions: Ask your child to break apart the following words into sounds. Do not show them the page.

Blot   Clap

Blank   Clip

Blur   Clan

Tap it Out

Ask your student to use their finger to tap each circle below each letter of the word as they make it's sound. Then, blend each sound together while they slide their finger over the arrow.

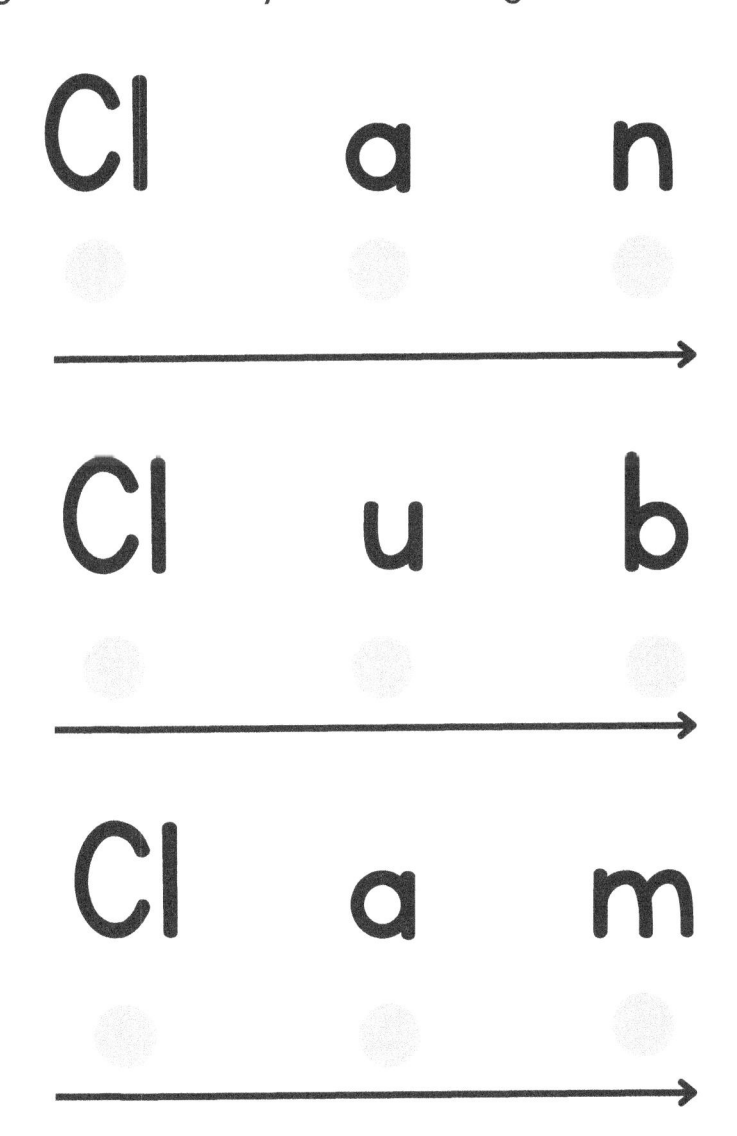

Cl a n

Cl u b

Cl a m

Tap it Out-2

Ask your student to use their finger to tap each circle below each letter of the word as they make it's sound. Then, blend each sound together while they slide their finger over the arrow.

Bl e ss

→

Bl a ck

→

Bl o b

→

Read
Read
Read

Directions: Ask the student to read the following sentences.

The clock will click.

Bob the black blob.

The clam is in the class.

Directions: Ask the student to read the text and color the picture after they are done reading.

The clam is in the sand. It claps and clinks. The clam can blab big talk to the blob. The blob will blink in class. The clam will clap, clap, clap by the cliff! The clam will blink for his blog.

What's that Word?

Directions: Ask your child to write a letter to create a new word. After they write the letter, read the whole word aloud.

Cl a __   Blo __

Bl __ e   __ l ass

C __ ap   Blo __

Card Flip Fun!

Directions: Cut out the cards and place them face down. Take turns flipping the cards over saying the word within five seconds.

Blog	Club
Clap	Blink
Blob	Blue

First to the Finish

Find a partner. Get a 6 sided die and two make-shift game pieces like a penny or a bead. Take turns rolling the die. Say the word you land on. The first to make it to the finish is the winner.

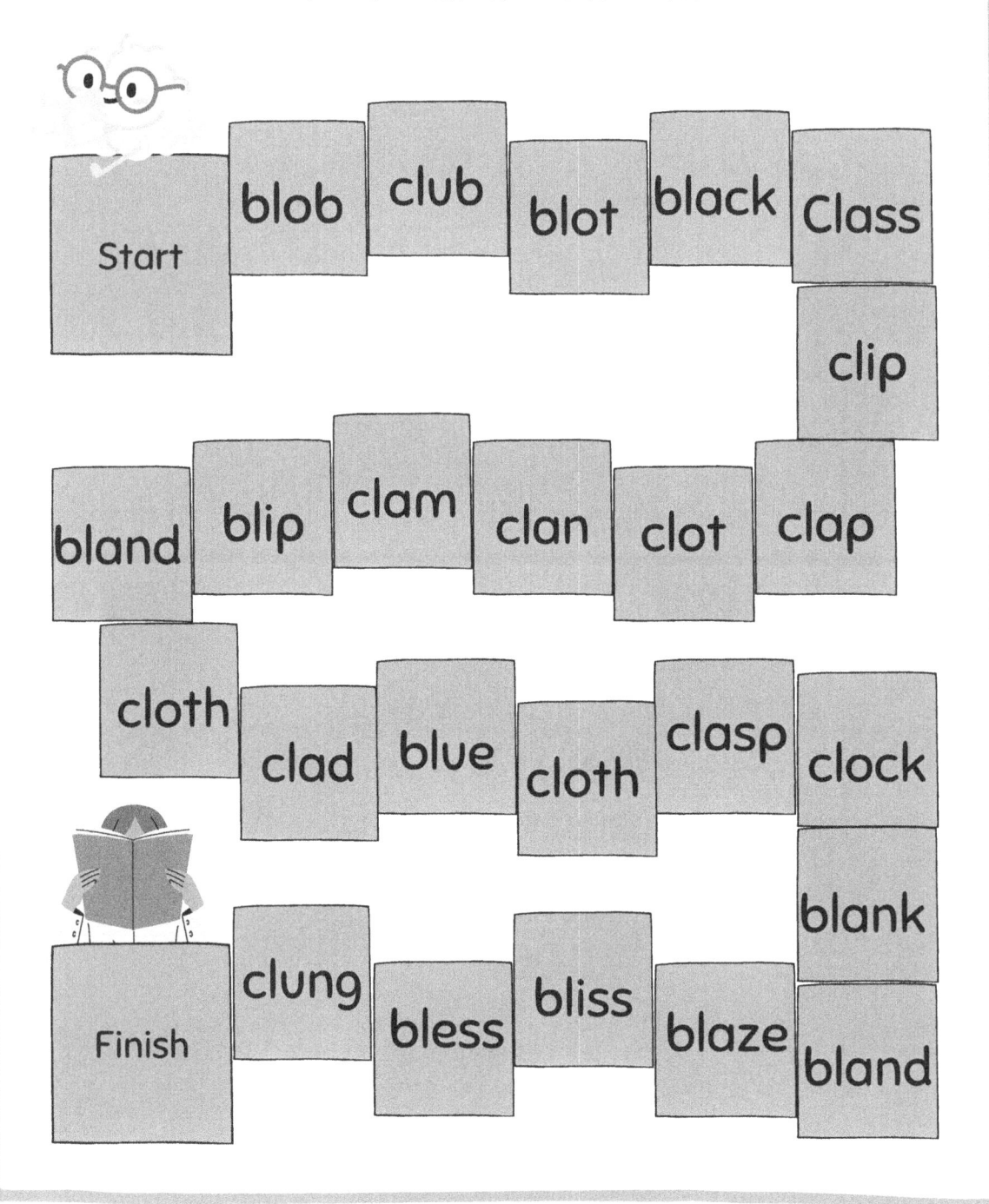

Start → blob → club → blot → black → Class → clip → clap → clot → clan → clam → blip → bland → cloth → clad → blue → cloth → clasp → clock → blank → bland → blaze → bliss → bless → clung → Finish

Name: Class:

SET 2
BLEND BL AND CL

Digraph BL, CL Sounds

What's that Sound?

Ask your child to isolate the beginning, middle, or final sound in each word. Alternate each day and adjust the lesson to your student's needs. Do not allow them to see the words or the book while doing this exercise.

Clip	Black
Clue	Bland
Clay	Blaze

Blending Sounds

Directions: Ask your child to blend the following sounds into words. Do not show them the page.

Cl-i-p   Bl-o-t

Cl-a-y   Bl-i-p

Cl-o-t   Bl-i-n-k

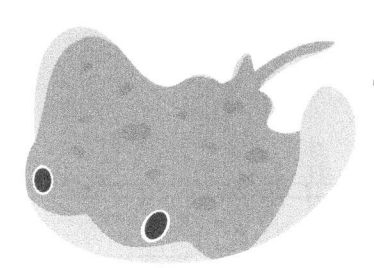

Segmenting Sounds

Directions: Ask your child to break apart the following words into sounds. Do not show them the page.

Blink   Clock

Bleep   Claim

Blind   Cloak

Tap it Out

Ask your student to use their finger to tap each circle below each letter of the word as they make it's sound. Then, blend each sound together while they slide their finger over the arrow.

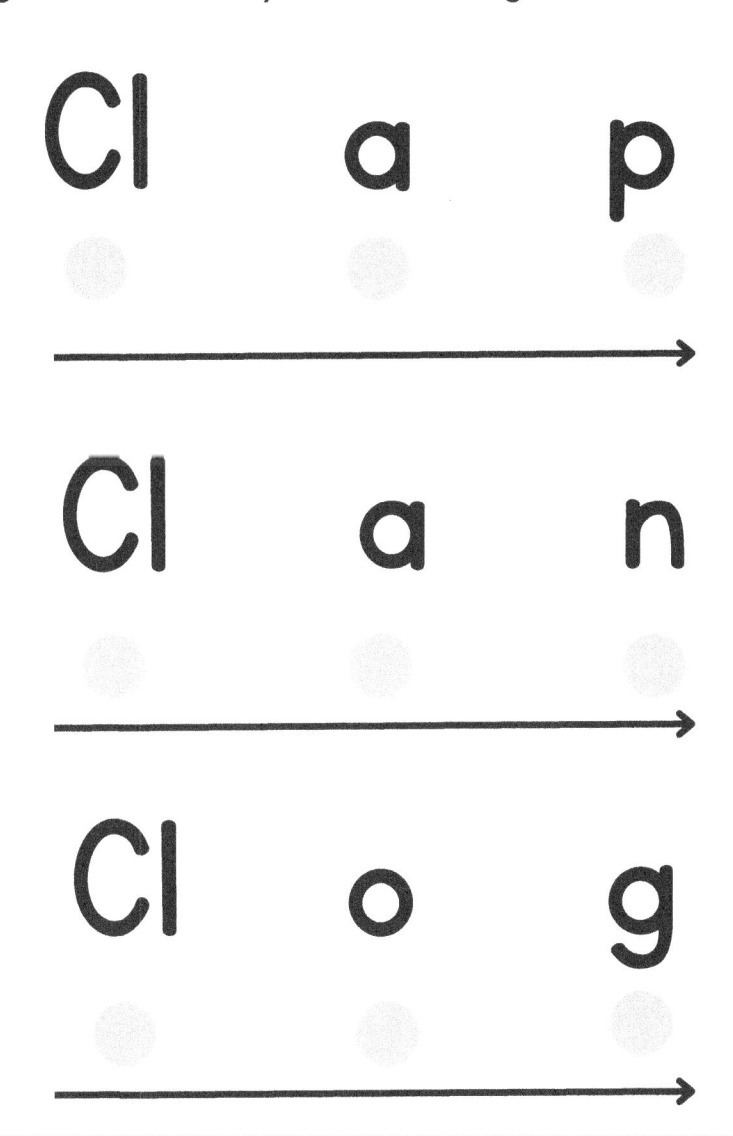

Cl a p

⟶

Cl a n

⟶

Cl o g

⟶

Tap it Out-2

Ask your student to use their finger to tap each circle below each letter of the word as they make it's sound. Then, blend each sound together while they slide their finger over the arrow.

Bl   i   p

→

Bl   i   n   k

→

Bl   o   t

→

Read
Read
Read

Directions: Ask the student to read the following sentences.

The cloth has a blue cap.

The Clam clips the cloth.

The black block is flat.

Directions: Ask the student to read the text and color the picture after they are done reading.

The cloth is black. It is blank and it can flap. The cloth will clip on my back. It is bland and long. The cloth will blend in with the clock. I clap as the cloth clung.

What's that Word?

Directions: Ask your child to write a letter to create a new word. After they write the letter, read the whole word aloud.

B l u __   C l a __

B l __ b   __ l a c k

b __ o b   C l a __

Card Flip Fun!

Directions: Cut out the cards and place them face down. Take turns flipping the cards over saying the word within five seconds.

Click	Blab
Clock	Blink
Cloth	Black

First to the Finish

Find a partner. Get a 6 sided die and two make-shift game pieces like a penny or a bead. Take turns rolling the die. Say the word you land on. The first to make it to the finish is the winner.

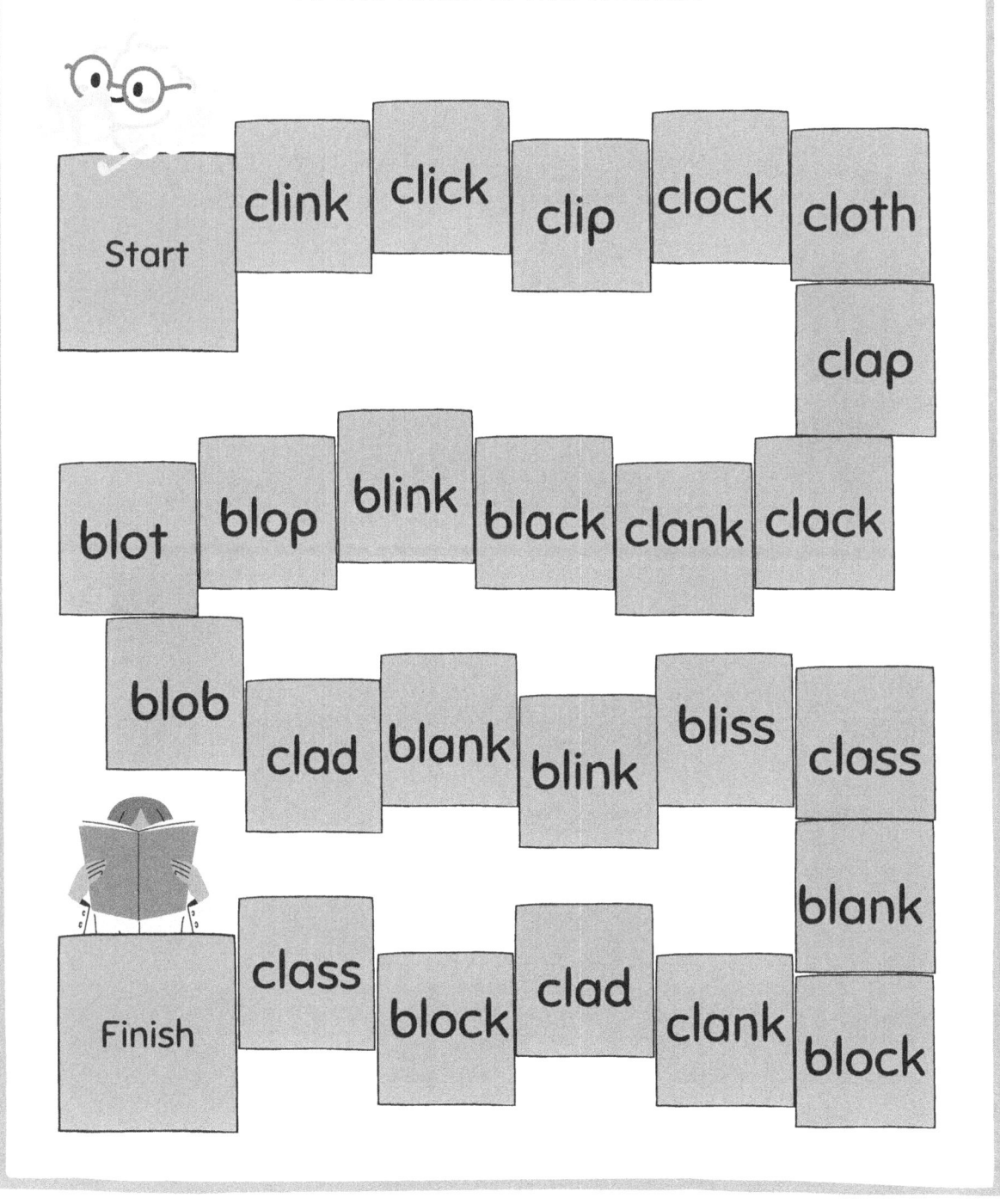

Start → clink → click → clip → clock → cloth → clap → clack → clank → black → blink → blop → blot → blob → clad → blank → blink → bliss → class → blank → block → clank → clad → block → class → Finish

Name: Class:

SET 3
BLEND BL AND CL

Digraph BL, CL Sounds

What's that Sound?

Ask your child to isolate the beginning, middle, or final sound in each word. Alternate each day and adjust the lesson to your student's needs. Do not allow them to see the words or the book while doing this exercise.

Clerk   Blown

Cling   Bluff

Clown   Blade

Blending Sounds

Directions: Ask your child to blend the following sounds into words. Do not show them the page.

Cl-a-d   Bl-i-n-g

Cl-i-c-k   Bl-e-s-s

Cl-o-t   Bl-i-s-s

Segmenting Sounds

Directions: Ask your child to break apart the following words into sounds. Do not show them the page.

Blown   Cling

Blank   Clamp

Block   Clash

Tap it Out

Ask your student to use their finger to tap each circle below each letter of the word as they make it's sound. Then, blend each sound together while they slide their finger over the arrow.

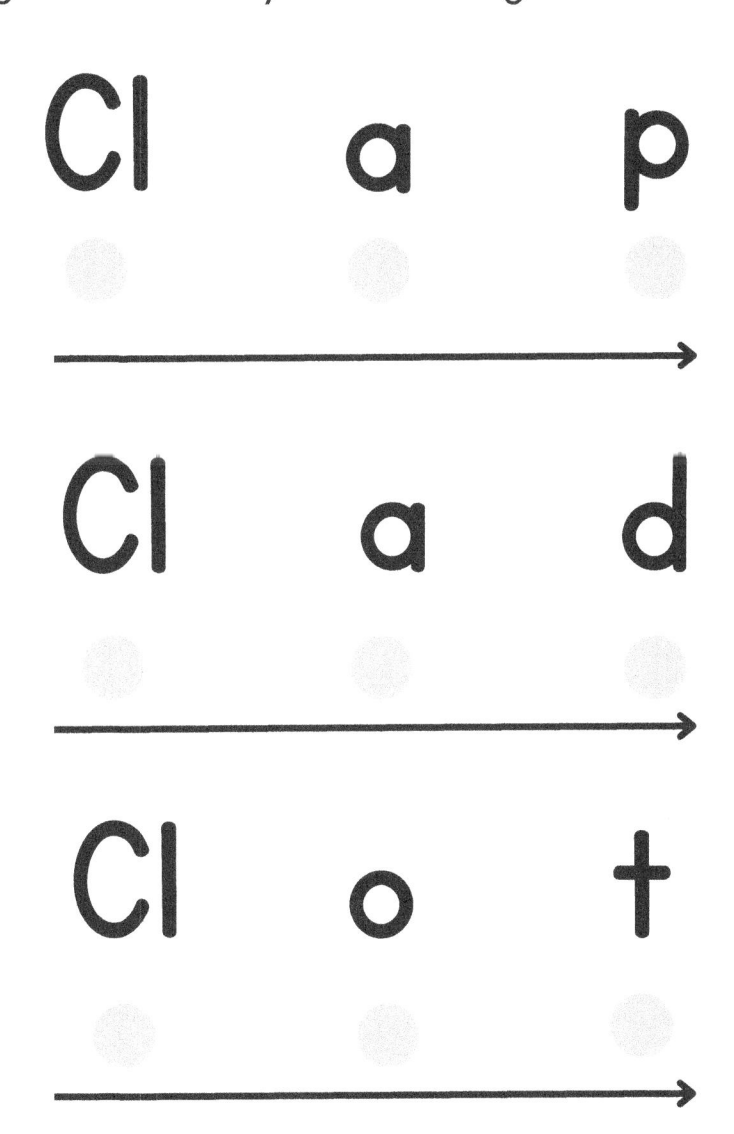

Cl a p

Cl a d

Cl o t

Tap it Out-2

Ask your student to use their finger to tap each circle below each letter of the word as they make it's sound. Then, blend each sound together while they slide their finger over the arrow.

Bl o p

Bl a s t

Bl u sh

Read
Read
Read

Directions: Ask the student to read the following sentences.

The clock is on the cloth.

Tom will clap and blink.

The blue blob can clash.

Directions: Ask the student to read the text and color the picture after they are done reading.

The blob is bland and blue. It can blink and clap. The blob will clinch and clench. It will blab and clap on the cliff. The blob will play. Clap, clap! The blob is glad.

What's that Word?

Directions: Ask your child to write a letter to create a new word. After they write the letter, read the whole word aloud.

Bl a __   Cl o __

Cl __ nch   __ l o b

C __ a n   Cl i __

Card Flip Fun!

Directions: Cut out the cards and place them face down. Take turns flipping the cards over saying the word within five seconds.

Cloth	Blend
Cliff	Blab
Clamp	Clench

First to the Finish

Find a partner. Get a 6 sided die and two make-shift game pieces like a penny or a bead. Take turns rolling the die. Say the word you land on. The first to make it to the finish is the winner.

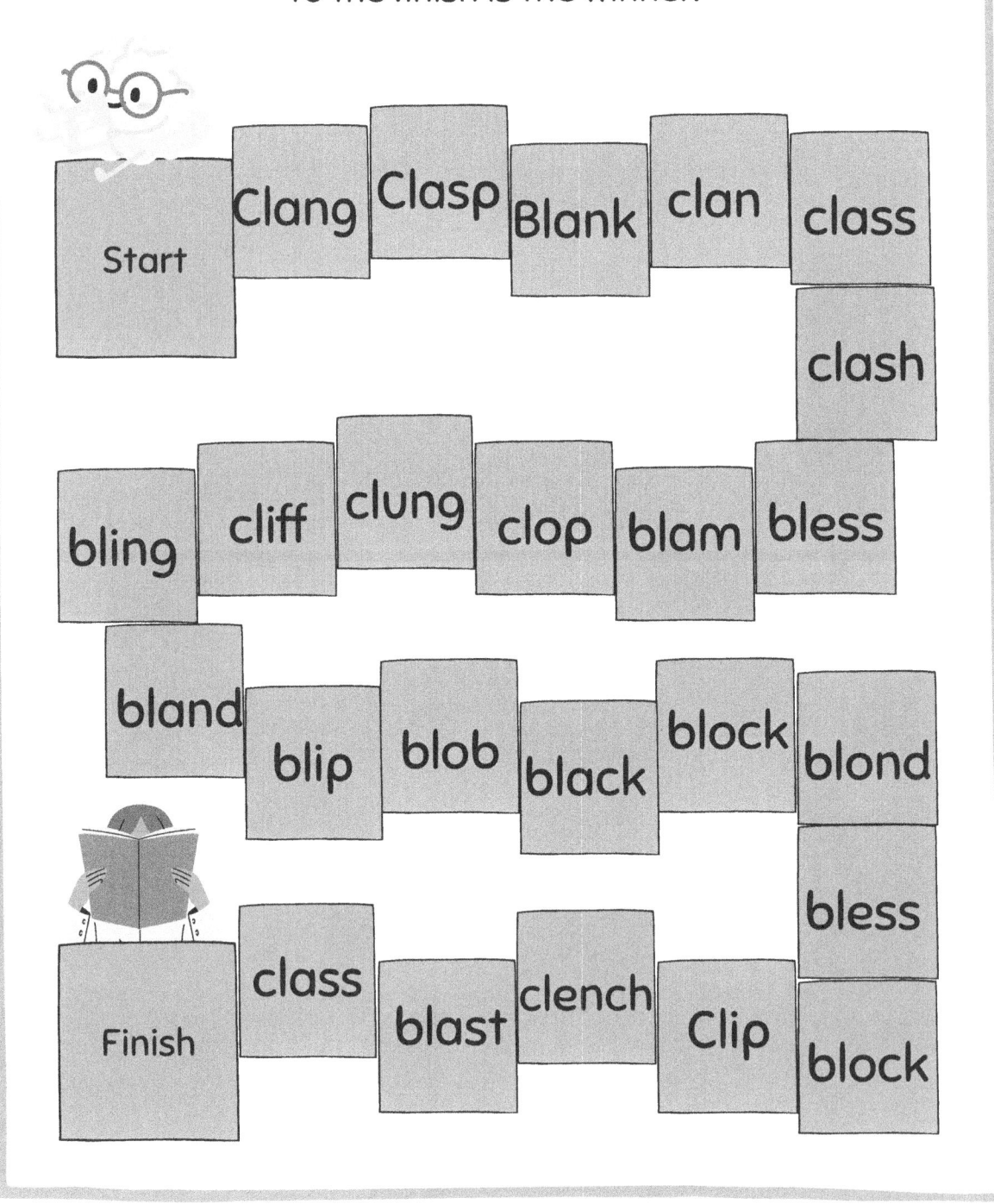

Start → Clang → Clasp → Blank → clan → class → clash → bless → blam → clop → clung → cliff → bling → bland → blip → blob → black → block → blond → bless → block → Clip → clench → blast → class → Finish

Name: Class:

SET 1
BLEND FL AND GL

Digraph Fl, Gl Sounds

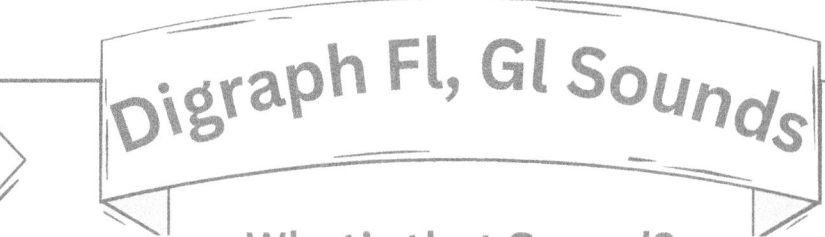

What's that Sound?

Ask your child to isolate the beginning, middle, or final sound in each word. Alternate each day and adjust the lesson to your student's needs. Do not allow them to see the words or the book while doing this exercise.

Fly	Glad
Flee	Glow
Flag	Glam

Blending Sounds

Directions: Ask your child to blend the following sounds into words. Do not show them the page.

Fl-ee	Gl-a-m

Fl-a-g	Gl-ue

Fl-a-p	Gl-ow

Segmenting Sounds

Directions: Ask your child to break apart the following words into sounds. Do not show them the page.

Glade　　Flat

Glaze　　Flop

Glint　　Flew

Tap it Out

Ask your student to use their finger to tap each circle below each letter of the word as they make it's sound. Then, blend each sound together while they slide their finger over the arrow.

Gl a d

Gl e n

Gl o ss

Tap it Out-2

Ask your student to use their finger to tap each circle below each letter of the word as they make it's sound. Then, blend each sound together while they slide their finger over the arrow.

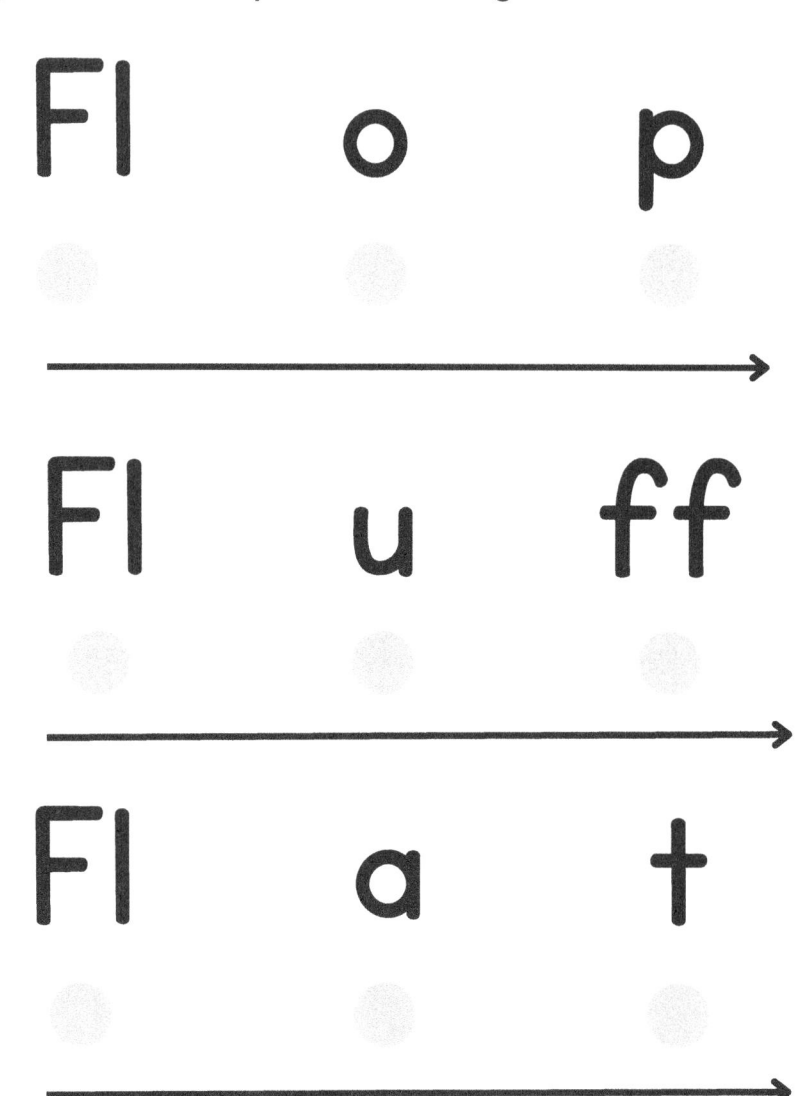

Fl o p

———————→

Fl u ff

———————→

Fl a t

———————→

Read
Read
Read

Directions: Ask the student to read the following sentences.

Glen will go up the hill.

Flip the big flag.

The glass is flat.

Directions: Ask the student to read the text and color the picture after they are done reading.

Flip got a flag. The flag is red and big. Flip will run fast and let the flag flap. Glen sees the flag. Glen will run to Flip. They like the flag and grin. Flip and Glen are glad!

What's that Word?

Directions: Ask your child to write a letter to create a new word. After they write the letter, read the whole word aloud.

Gl a __   Gl e __

Fl __ g   __ l a d

F __ a t   Fl o __

Card Flip Fun!

Directions: Cut out the cards and place them face down. Take turns flipping the cards over saying the word within five seconds.

Flag	Glad
Flip	Flex
Glen	Glass

First to the Finish

Find a partner. Get a 6 sided die and two make-shift game pieces like a penny or a bead. Take turns rolling the die. Say the word you land on. The first to make it to the finish is the winner.

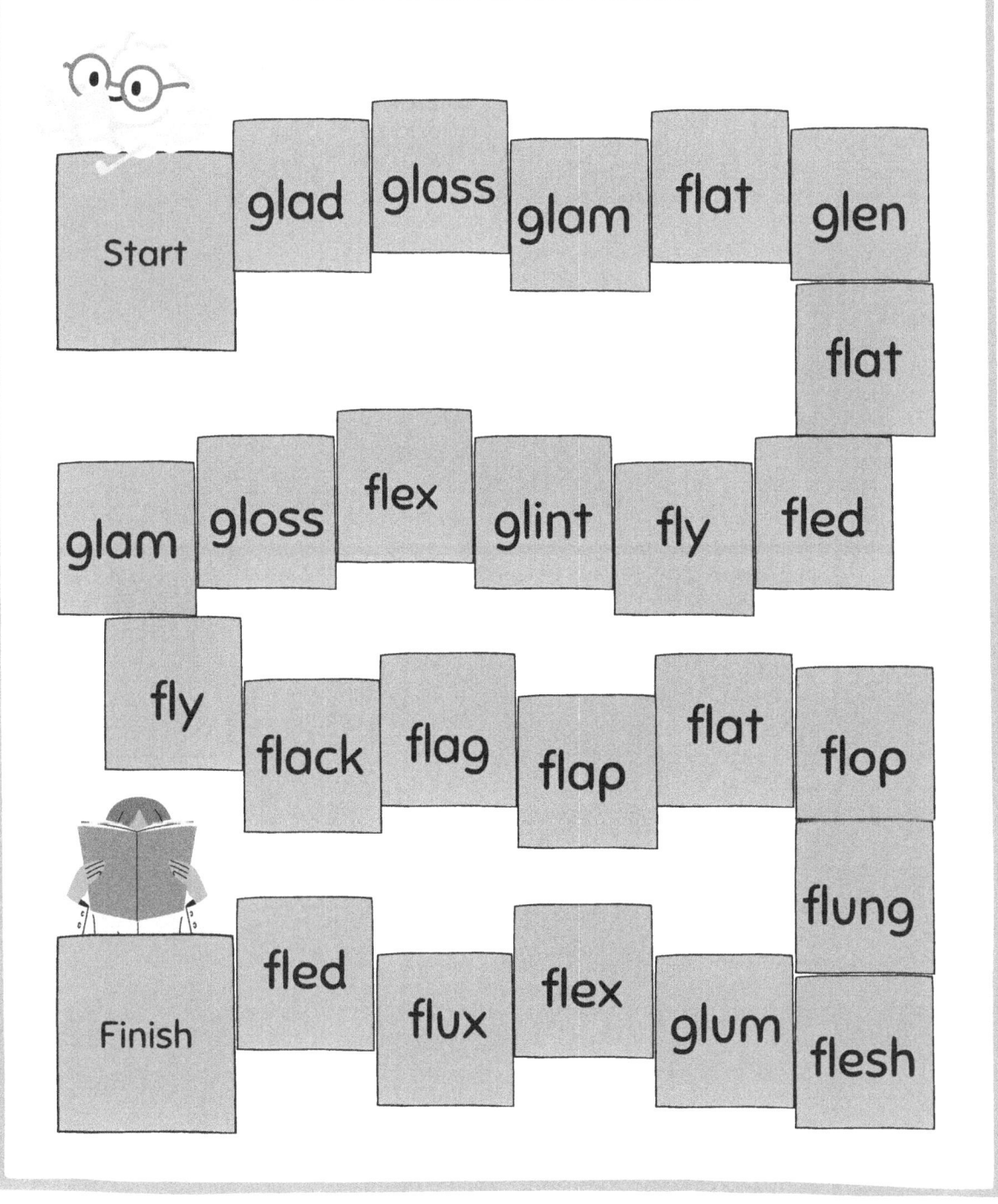

Start → glad → glass → glam → flat → glen → flat → fled → fly → glint → flex → gloss → glam → fly → flack → flag → flap → flat → flop → flung → flesh → glum → flex → flux → fled → Finish

Name: Class:

SET 2
BLEND FL AND GL

Digraph Fl, Gl Sounds

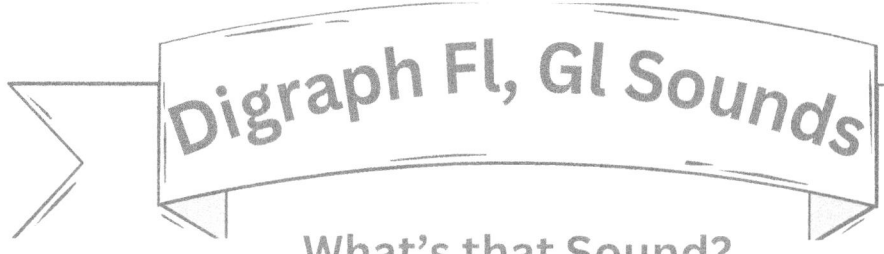

What's that Sound?

Ask your child to isolate the beginning, middle, or final sound in each word. Alternate each day and adjust the lesson to your student's needs. Do not allow them to see the words or the book while doing this exercise.

Glue	Flea
Glee	Flex
Glen	Flux

Blending Sounds

Directions: Ask your child to blend the following sounds into words. Do not show them the page.

Fl-e-d   Gl-ee

Fl-i-p   Gl-e-n

Fl-ow   Gl-ue

Segmenting Sounds

Directions: Ask your child to break apart the following words into sounds. Do not show them the page.

Globe   Flame

Gloss   Flash

Glide   Flush

Tap it Out

Ask your student to use their finger to tap each circle below each letter of the word as they make it's sound. Then, blend each sound together while they slide their finger over the arrow.

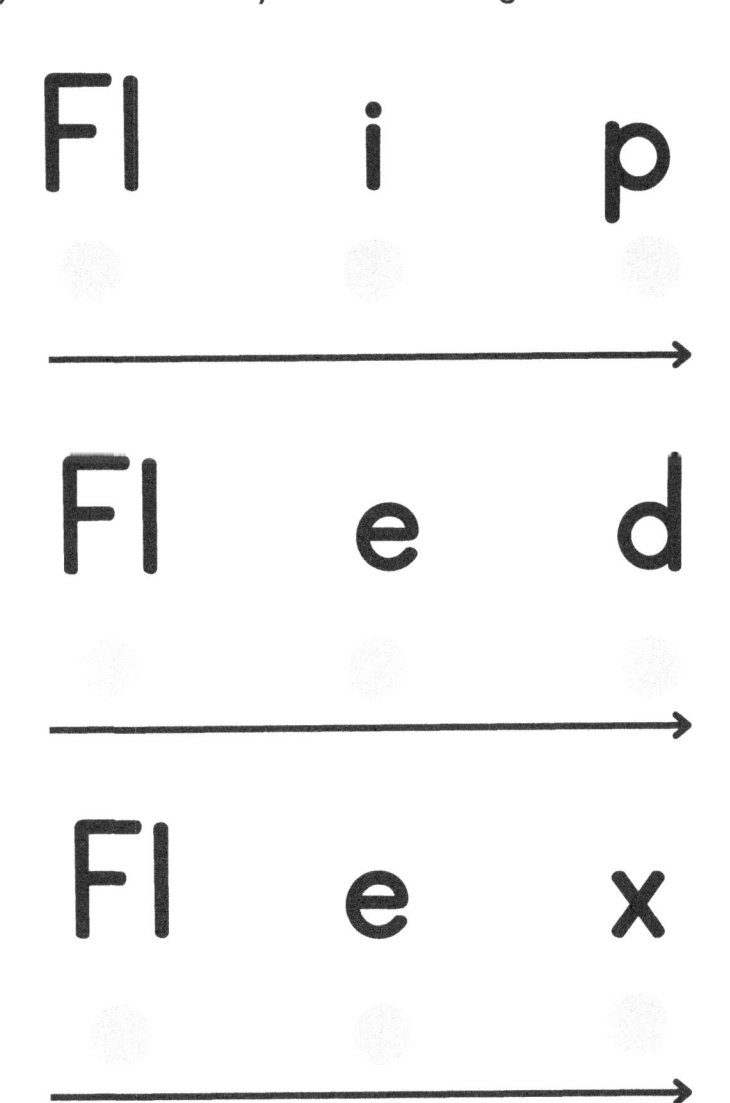

Fl   i   p

———————→

Fl   e   d

———————→

Fl   e   x

———————→

Tap it Out-2

Ask your student to use their finger to tap each circle below each letter of the word as they make it's sound. Then, blend each sound together while they slide their finger over the arrow.

Gl a d

Gl a n d

Gl e n

Read
Read
Read

Directions: Ask the student to read the following sentences.

The glass will not flip.

Glen had a flash stick.

I see a flock of ducks.

Directions: Ask the student to read the text and color the picture after they are done reading.

Flon had a glum bug on her hat. The bug did a flip and Flon was glad. Flon and the bug hop fast. The glum bug flaps to fly. The bug can fly, then Flon can flank her by the flock of ducks.

What's that Word?

Directions: Ask your child to write a letter to create a new word. After they write the letter, read the whole word aloud.

F l e __   G l e __

F l __ x   __ l u m

F __ i p   G l a __

Card Flip Fun!

Directions: Cut out the cards and place them face down. Take turns flipping the cards over saying the word within five seconds.

Glum	Flip
glad	Flock
Gloss	Fly

First to the Finish

Find a partner. Get a 6 sided die and two make-shift game pieces like a penny or a bead. Take turns rolling the die. Say the word you land on. The first to make it to the finish is the winner.

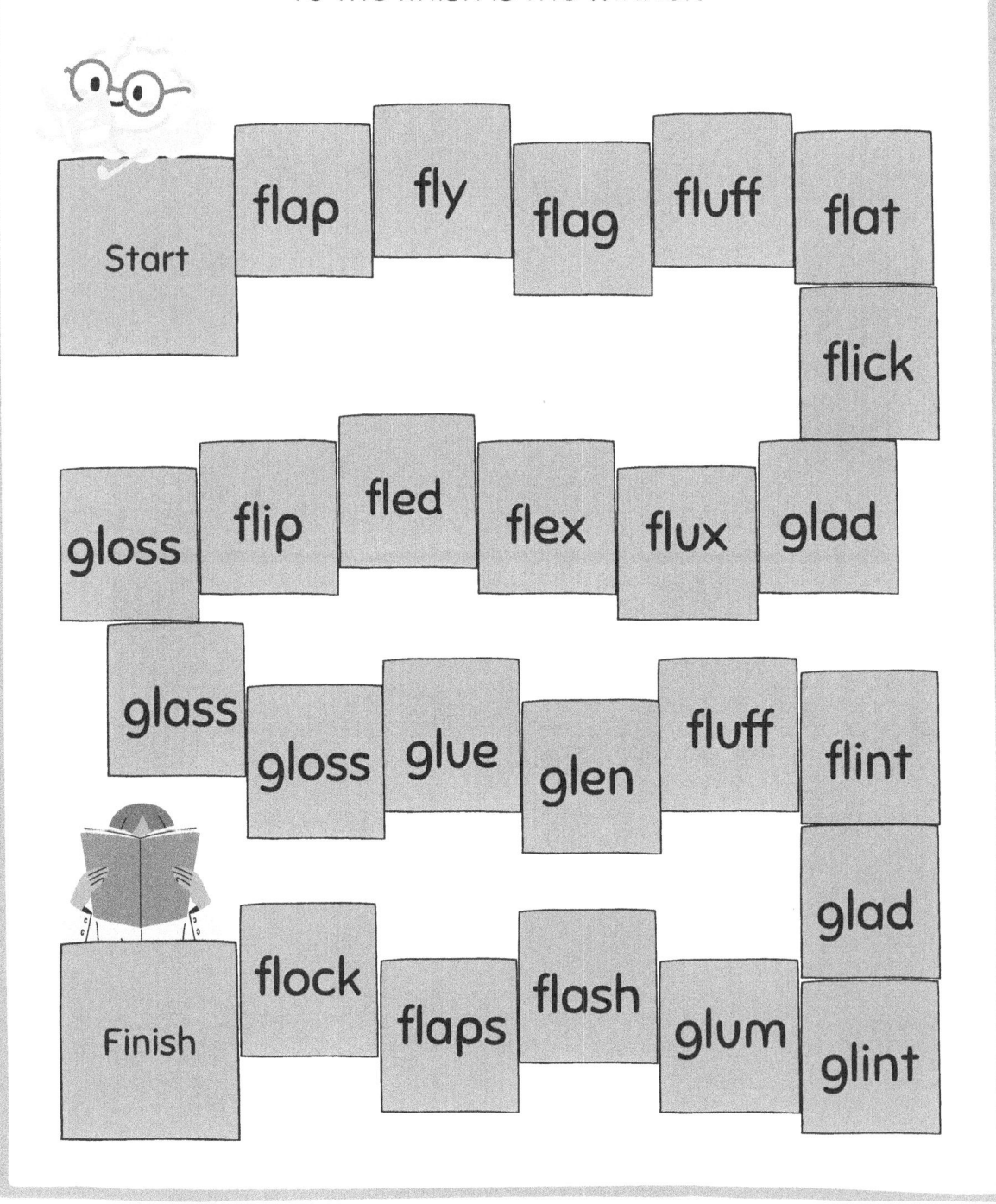

Start → flap → fly → flag → fluff → flat → flick → glad → flux → flex → fled → flip → gloss → glass → gloss → glue → glen → fluff → flint → glad → glint → glum → flash → flaps → flock → Finish

Name: Class:

SET 1
BLEND PL AND SL

Digraph Pl, Sl Sounds

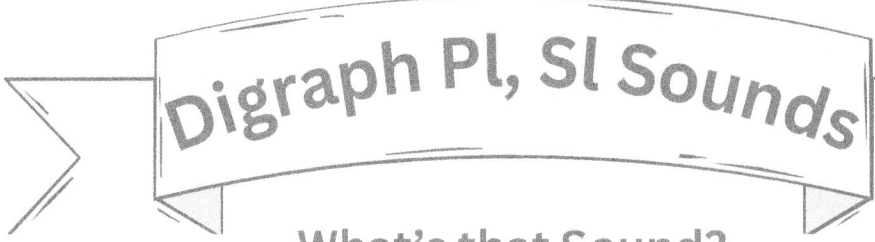

What's that Sound?

Ask your child to isolate the beginning, middle, or final sound in each word. Alternate each day and adjust the lesson to your student's needs. Do not allow them to see the words or the book while doing this exercise.

Ply   Sly

Plan   Slab

Plot   Slay

Blending Sounds

Directions: Ask your child to blend the following sounds into words. Do not show them the page.

Pl-a-n   Sl-i-m

Pl-o-t   Sl-ow

Pl-u-m   Sl-a-p

Segmenting Sounds

Directions: Ask your child to break apart the following words into sounds. Do not show them the page.

Sled   Plan

Slip   Plug

Slug   Plot

Tap it Out

Ask your student to use their finger to tap each circle below each letter of the word as they make it's sound. Then, blend each sound together while they slide their finger over the arrow.

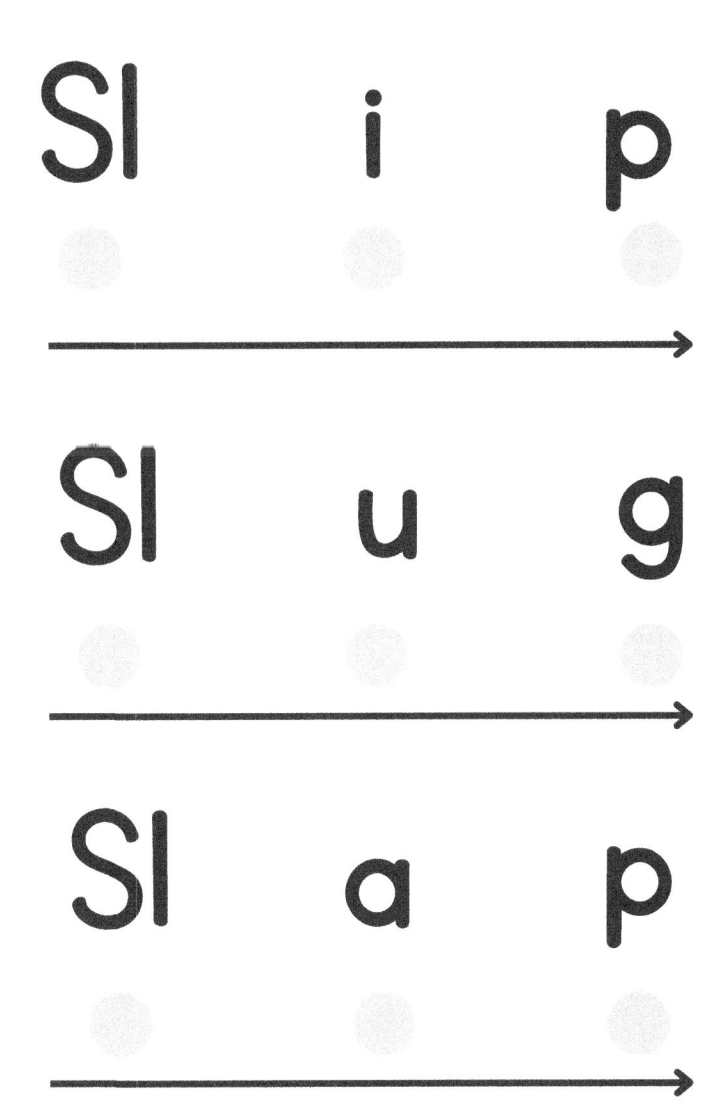

Sl   i   p

⟶

Sl   u   g

⟶

Sl   a   p

⟶

Tap it Out-2

Ask your student to use their finger to tap each circle below each letter of the word as they make it's sound. Then, blend each sound together while they slide their finger over the arrow.

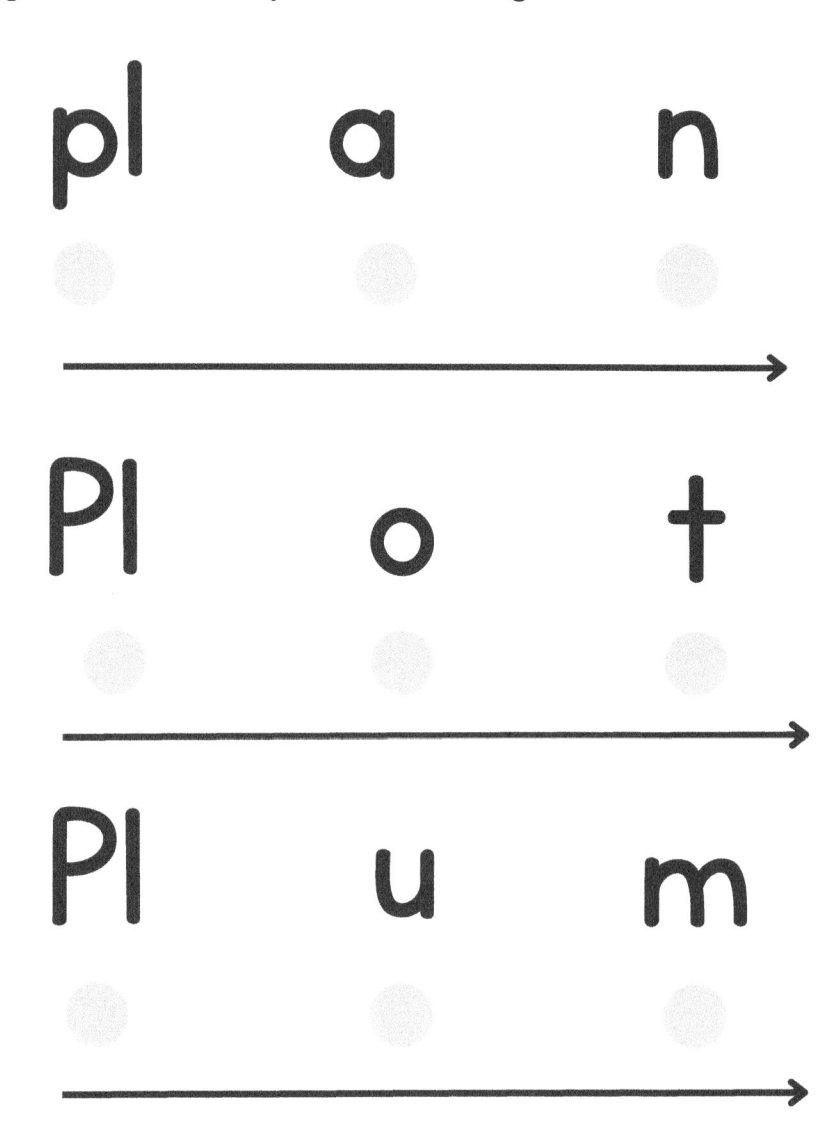

pl   a   n

Pl   o   t

Pl   u   m

Read
Read
Read

Directions: Ask the student to read the following sentences.

The slug slid on the path.

Pam will plant the plum.

The sled is on the hill.

Directions: Ask the student to read the text and color the picture after they are done reading.

Slim saw a plum on the hill. He will pluck the plum and slip it in his bag. The plum is big and red. Slim has a bit and grins. The plum is plush! Slim plans to plant more.

What's that Word?

Directions: Ask your child to write a letter to create a new word. After they write the letter, read the whole word aloud.

Sl u __   Sl i __

Pl __ m   __ l an

S __ ap   Pl o __

Card Flip Fun!

Directions: Cut out the cards and place them face down. Take turns flipping the cards over saying the word within five seconds.

Ply	Slam
Slug	Plant
Slim	Plus

First to the Finish

Find a partner. Get a 6 sided die and two make-shift game pieces like a penny or a bead. Take turns rolling the die. Say the word you land on. The first to make it to the finish is the winner.

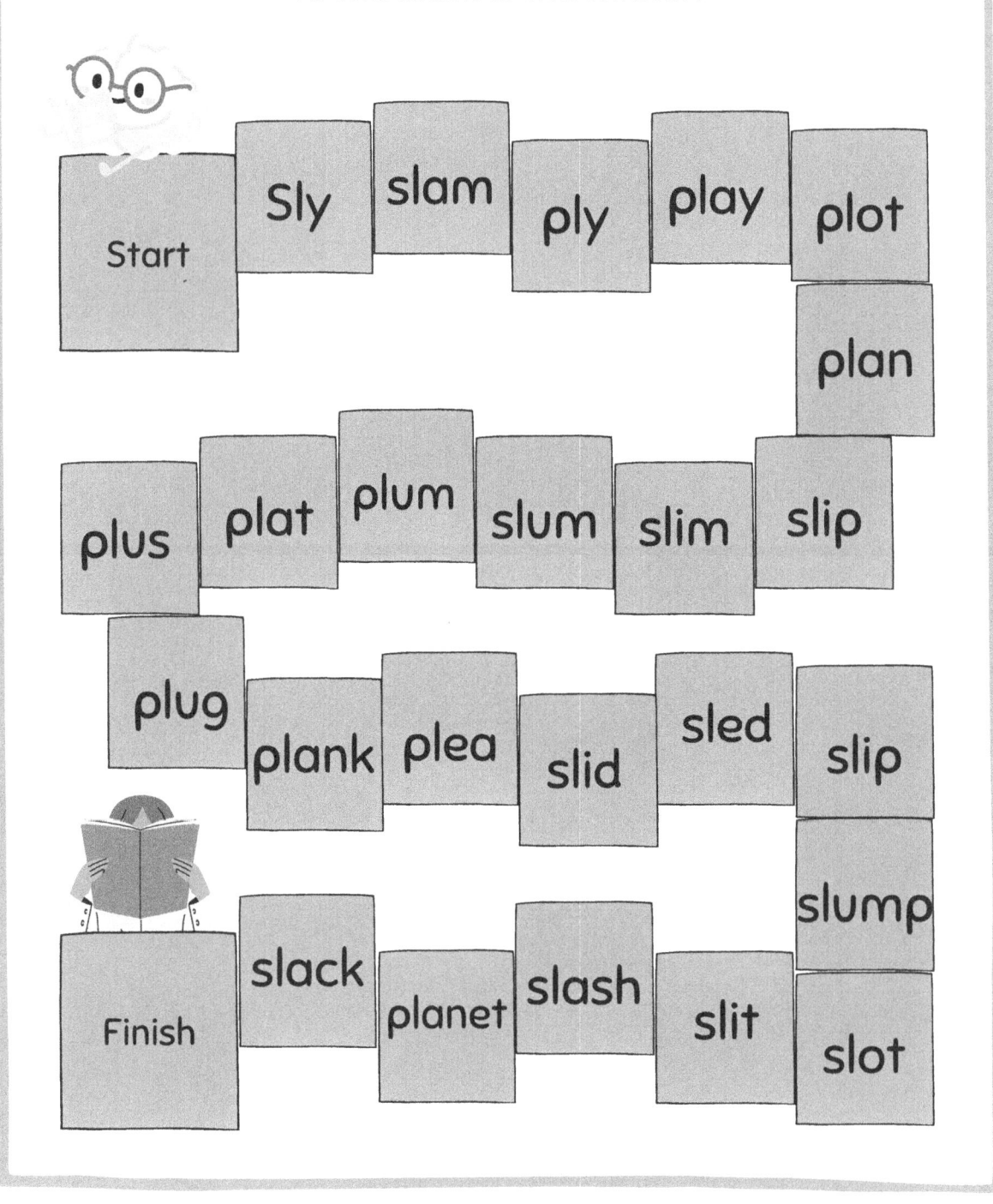

Start → Sly → slam → ply → play → plot → plan → slip → slim → slum → plum → plat → plus → plug → plank → plea → slid → sled → slip → slump → slot → slit → slash → planet → slack → Finish

Name: Class:

SET 2
BLEND PL AND SL

Digraph Pl, Sl Sounds

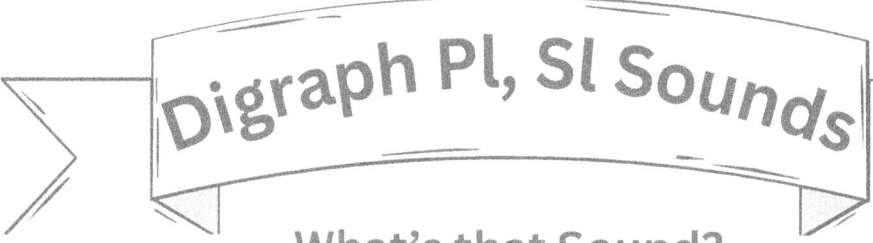

What's that Sound?

Ask your child to isolate the beginning, middle, or final sound in each word. Alternate each day and adjust the lesson to your student's needs. Do not allow them to see the words or the book while doing this exercise.

Slip   Plea

Slug   Plus

Slam   Plow

Blending Sounds

Directions: Ask your child to blend the following sounds into words. Do not show them the page.

Pl-ea   Sl-u-m

Pl-u-g   Sl-o-t

Pl-u-s   Sl-i-t

Segmenting Sounds

Directions: Ask your child to break apart the following words into sounds. Do not show them the page.

Slip   Pluck

Slid   Plan

Slump   Plant

Tap it Out

Ask your student to use their finger to tap each circle below each letter of the word as they make it's sound. Then, blend each sound together while they slide their finger over the arrow.

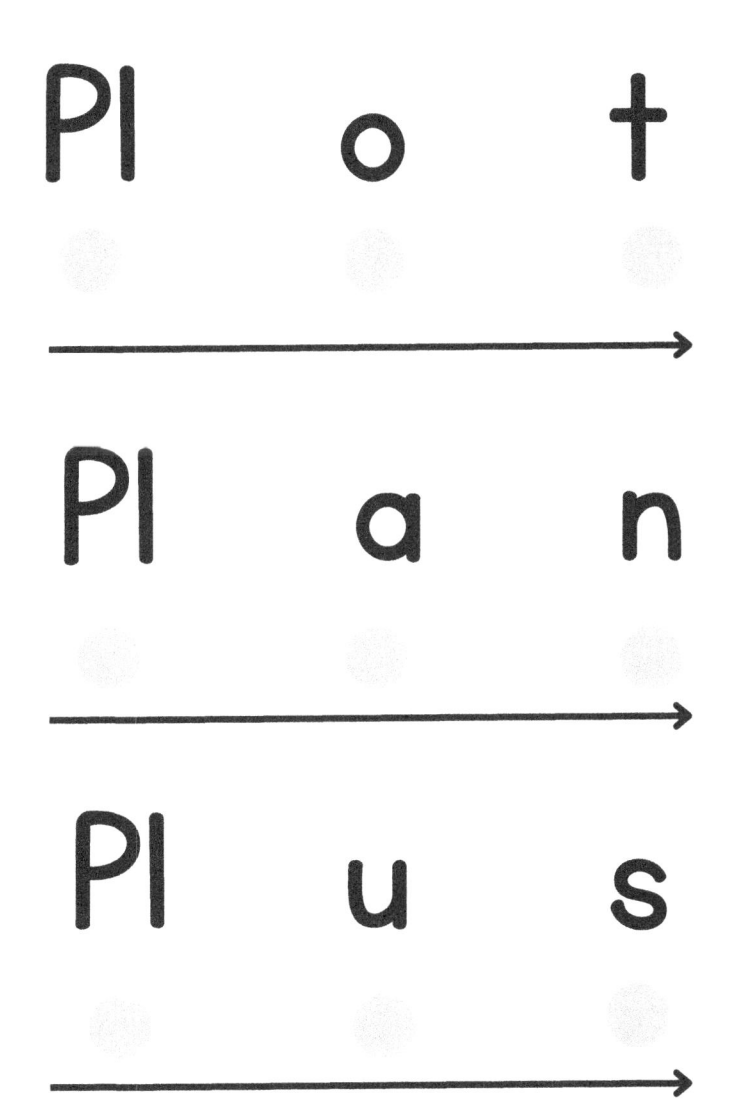

Pl o t

Pl a n

Pl u s

Tap it Out-2

Ask your student to use their finger to tap each circle below each letter of the word as they make it's sound. Then, blend each sound together while they slide their finger over the arrow.

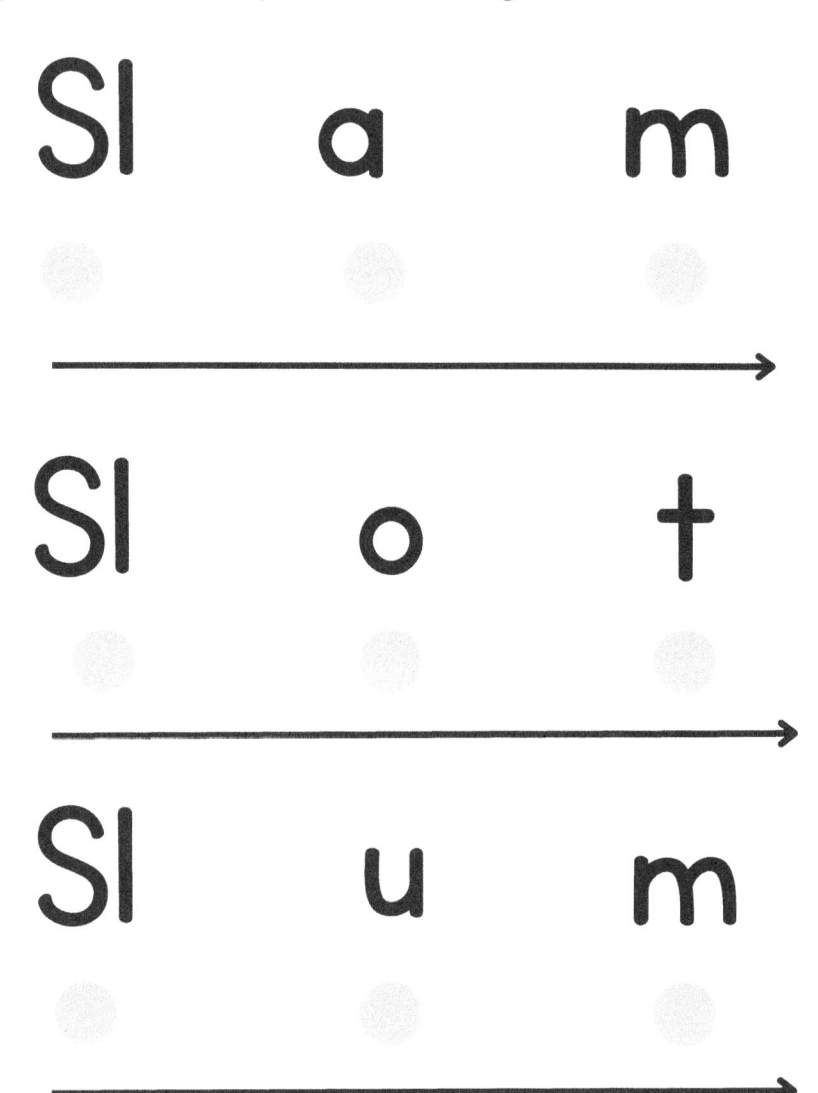

Sl   a   m

⎯⎯⎯⎯⎯⎯⎯⎯→

Sl   o   t

⎯⎯⎯⎯⎯⎯⎯⎯→

Sl   u   m

⎯⎯⎯⎯⎯⎯⎯⎯→

Read
Read
Read

Directions: Ask the student to read the following sentences.

The plug is in the slot.

I will cut the plum.

The plan will slip fast.

Directions: Ask the student to read the text and color the picture after they are done reading.

Sam saw a slug in the mud. The slug slid by a plant. Sam will pluck the slug on a flat rock. The slug is slick and slim. Sam is sly and the slug slips off the rock and onto a plush slump.

What's that Word?

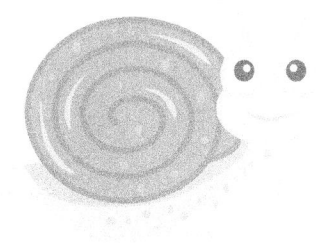

Directions: Ask your child to write a letter to create a new word.
After they write the letter, read the whole word aloud.

Sli __   Sla __

Pl __ n   __ luck

S __ ap   Slu __

Card Flip Fun!

Directions: Cut out the cards and place them face down. Take turns flipping the cards over saying the word within five seconds.

Sled	Plot
Slum	Plan
Slack	Plug

First to the Finish

Find a partner. Get a 6 sided die and two make-shift game pieces like a penny or a bead. Take turns rolling the die. Say the word you land on. The first to make it to the finish is the winner.

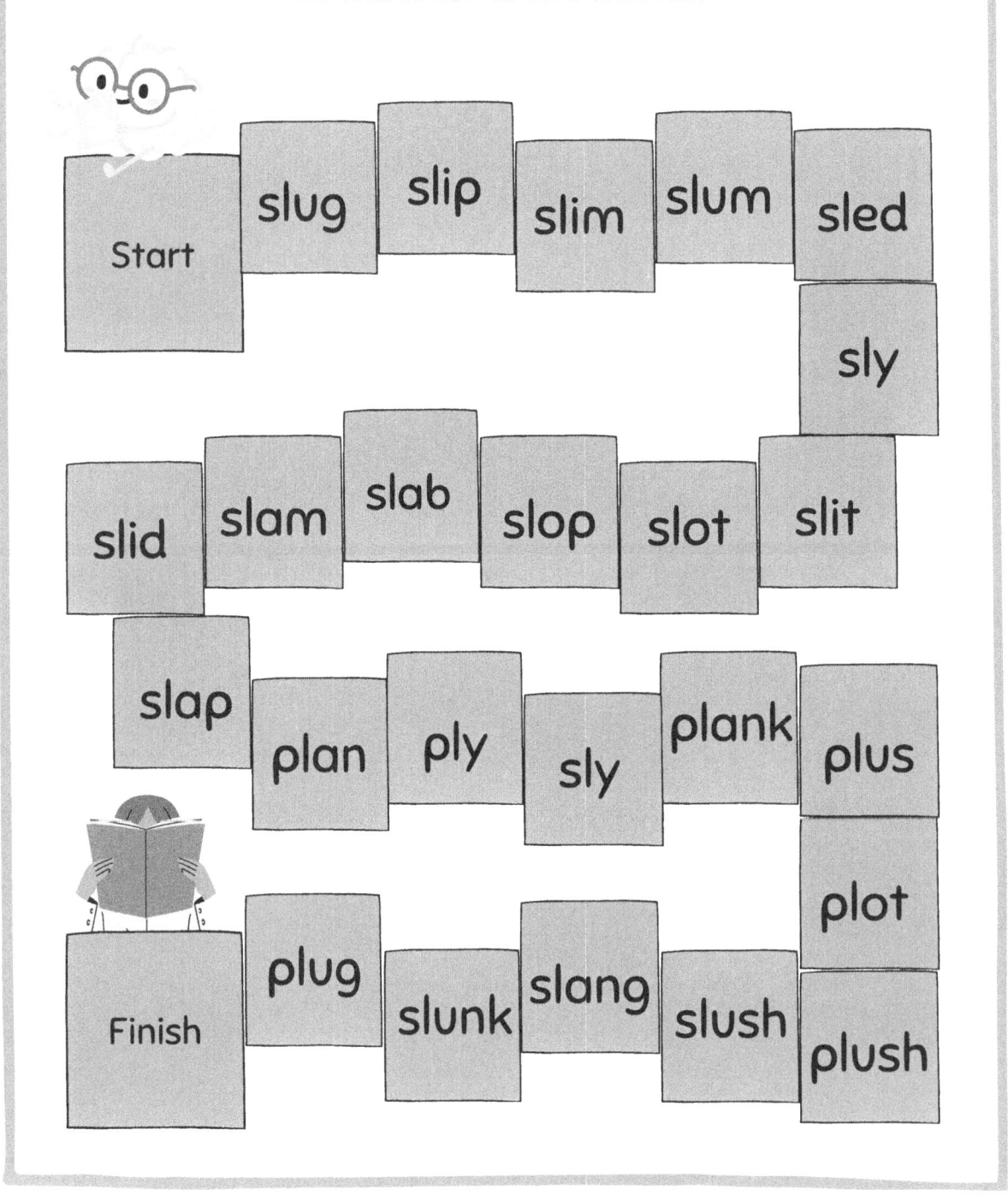

Start → slug → slip → slim → slum → sled → sly → slit → slot → slop → slab → slam → slid → slap → plan → ply → sly → plank → plus → plot → plush → slush → slang → slunk → plug → Finish

Name: Class:

SET 3
BLEND PL AND SL

Digraph Pl, Sl Sounds

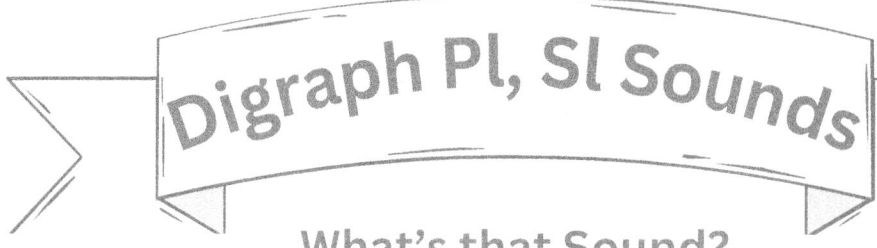

What's that Sound?

Ask your child to isolate the beginning, middle, or final sound in each word. Alternate each day and adjust the lesson to your student's needs. Do not allow them to see the words or the book while doing this exercise.

Ploy	Slash
Plain	Slope
Plead	Sleep

Blending Sounds

Directions: Ask your child to blend the following sounds into words. Do not show them the page.

Sl-i-t   Pl-oy

Sl-u-m   Pl-ea

Sl-e-d   Pl-ay

Segmenting Sounds

Directions: Ask your child to break apart the following words into sounds. Do not show them the page.

Slime   Plane

Sloth   Pluck

Sleep   Plump

Tap it Out

Ask your student to use their finger to tap each circle below each letter of the word as they make it's sound. Then, blend each sound together while they slide their finger over the arrow.

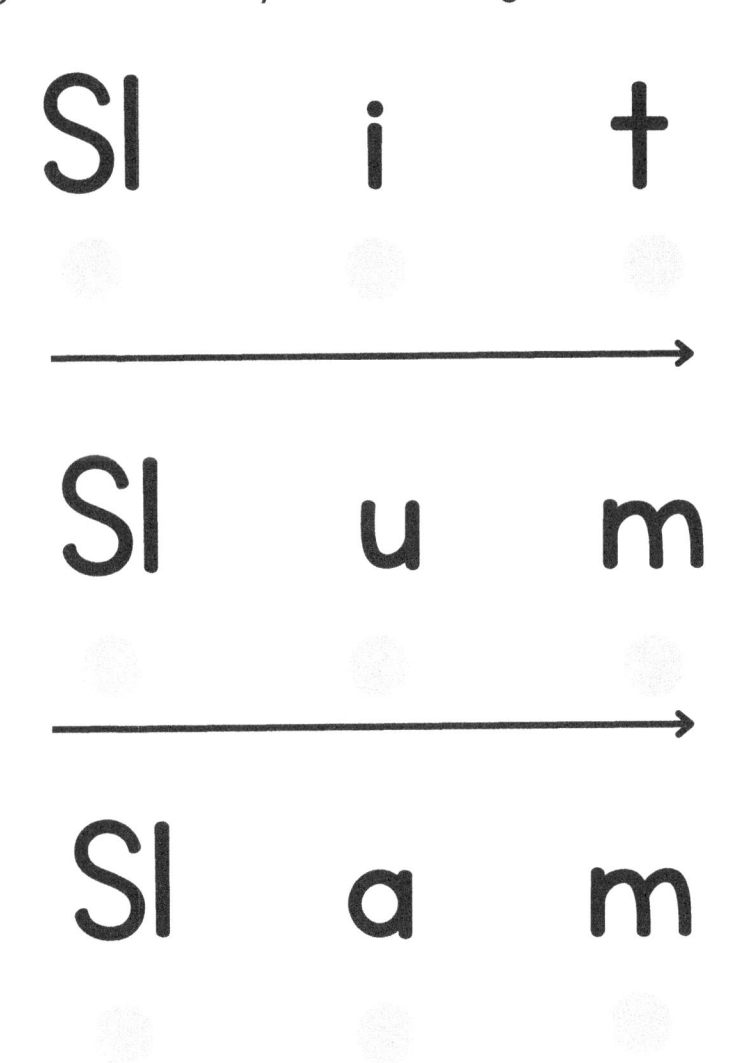

Sl i t

→

Sl u m

→

Sl a m

→

Tap it Out-2

Ask your student to use their finger to tap each circle below each letter of the word as they make it's sound. Then, blend each sound together while they slide their finger over the arrow.

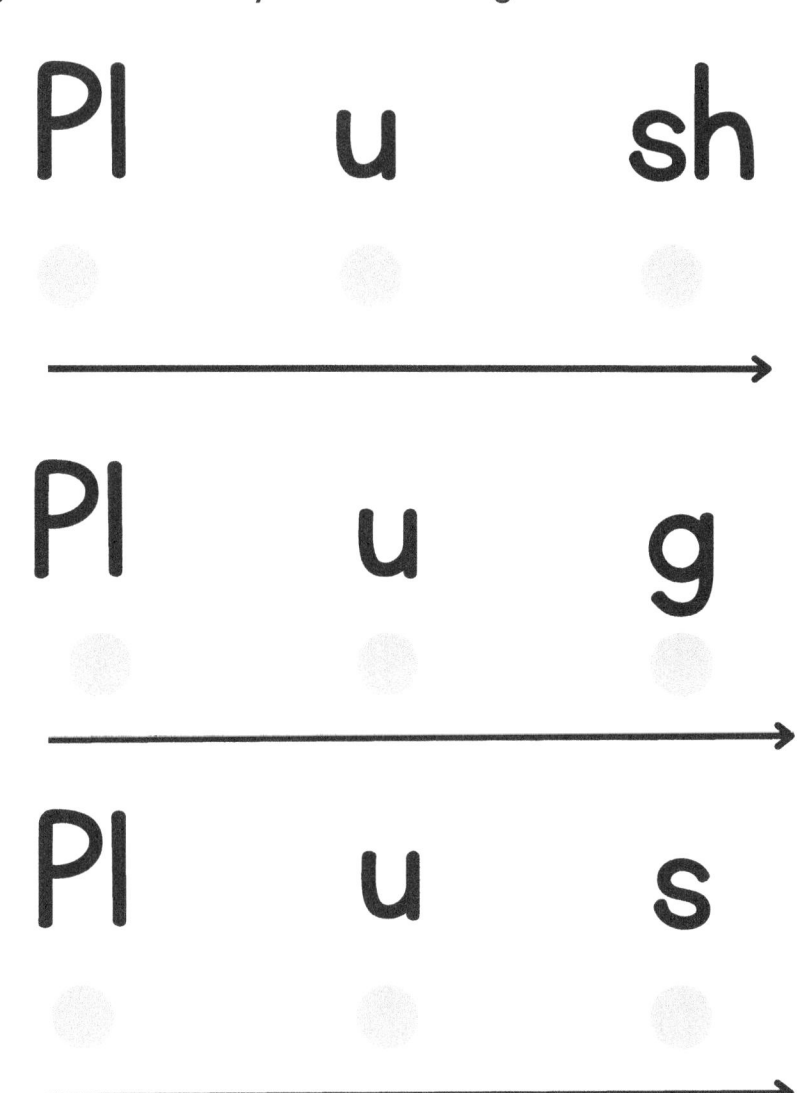

Pl u sh

Pl u g

Pl u s

Read
Read
Read

Directions: Ask the student to read the following sentences.

The sled will slip fast.

Pam will plant a plum.

The plug fits in the slot.

Directions: Ask the student to read the text and color the picture after they are done reading.

The sloth sits on a slim branch. It is slim and slips a bit. Pam sees the sloth and slams into it. She will put a plant by the sloth. The sloth likes the plant and naps. The slim sloth is glad!

What's that Word?

Directions: Ask your child to write a letter to create a new word. After they write the letter, read the whole word aloud.

Sl u __   Sli __

Pl __ m   __ ly

S __ y   Slo __

Card Flip Fun!

Directions: Cut out the cards and place them face down. Take turns flipping the cards over saying the word within five seconds.

Plank	Plot
Sloth	Plant
Slim	Sly

First to the Finish

Find a partner. Get a 6 sided die and two make-shift game pieces like a penny or a bead. Take turns rolling the die. Say the word you land on. The first to make it to the finish is the winner.

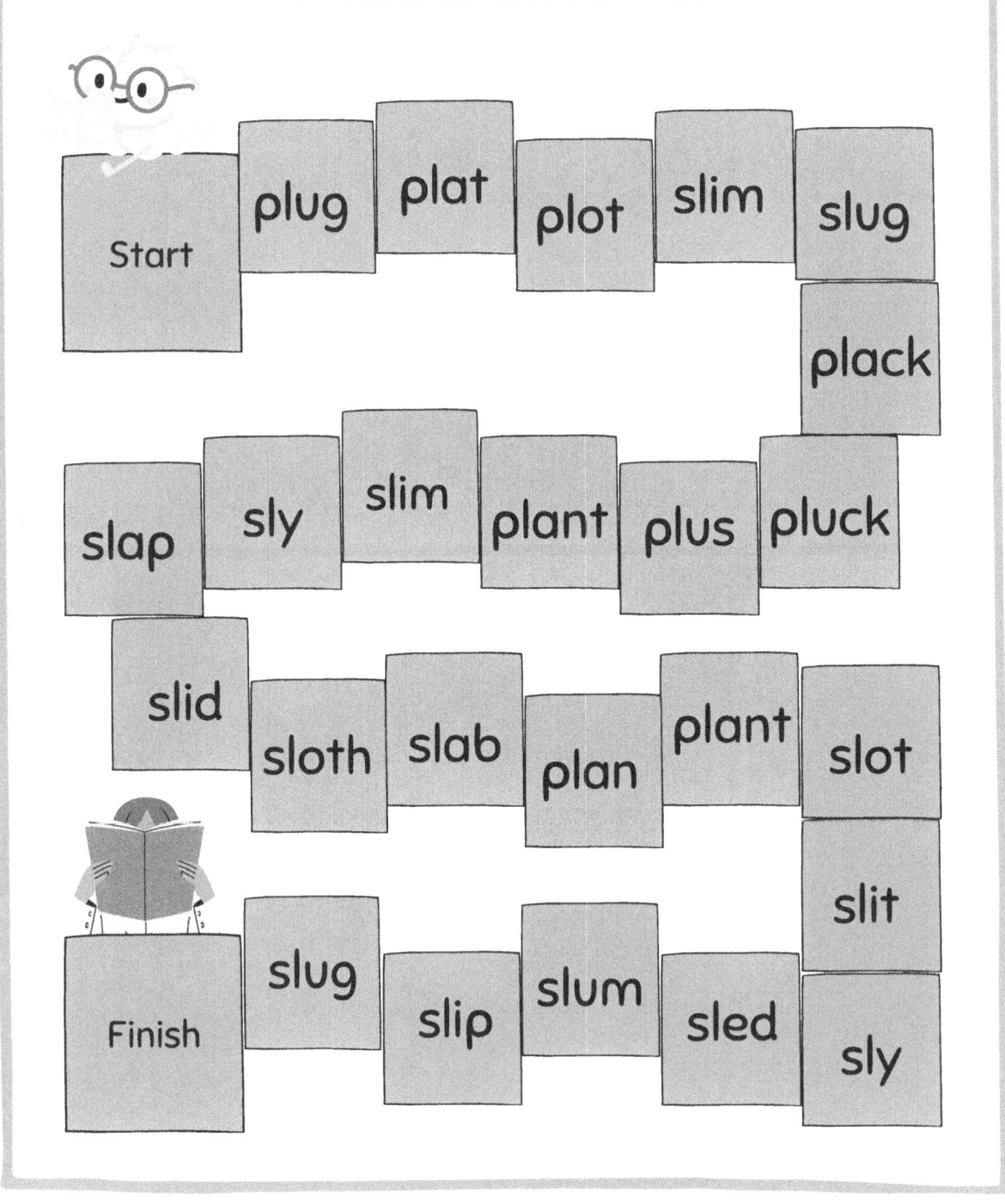

Start → plug → plat → plot → slim → slug → plack → pluck → plus → plant → slim → sly → slap → slid → sloth → slab → plan → plant → slot → slit → sly → sled → slum → slip → slug → Finish

Name: Class:

SET 1
BLEND BR AND CR

Digraph Br, Cr Sounds

What's that Sound?

Ask your child to isolate the beginning, middle, or final sound in each word. Alternate each day and adjust the lesson to your student's needs. Do not allow them to see the words or the book while doing this exercise.

Brag	**Cry**
Brew	**Crab**
Bring	**Crib**

Blending Sounds

Directions: Ask your child to blend the following sounds into words. Do not show them the page.

Cr-a-m   Br-a-n

Cr-o-p   Br-i-m

Cr-a-b   Br-o-w

Segmenting Sounds

Directions: Ask your child to break apart the following words into sounds. Do not show them the page.

Brain   Crawl

Crown   Brass

Brawn   Crash

Tap it Out

Ask your student to use their finger to tap each circle below each letter of the word as they make it's sound. Then, blend each sound together while they slide their finger over the arrow.

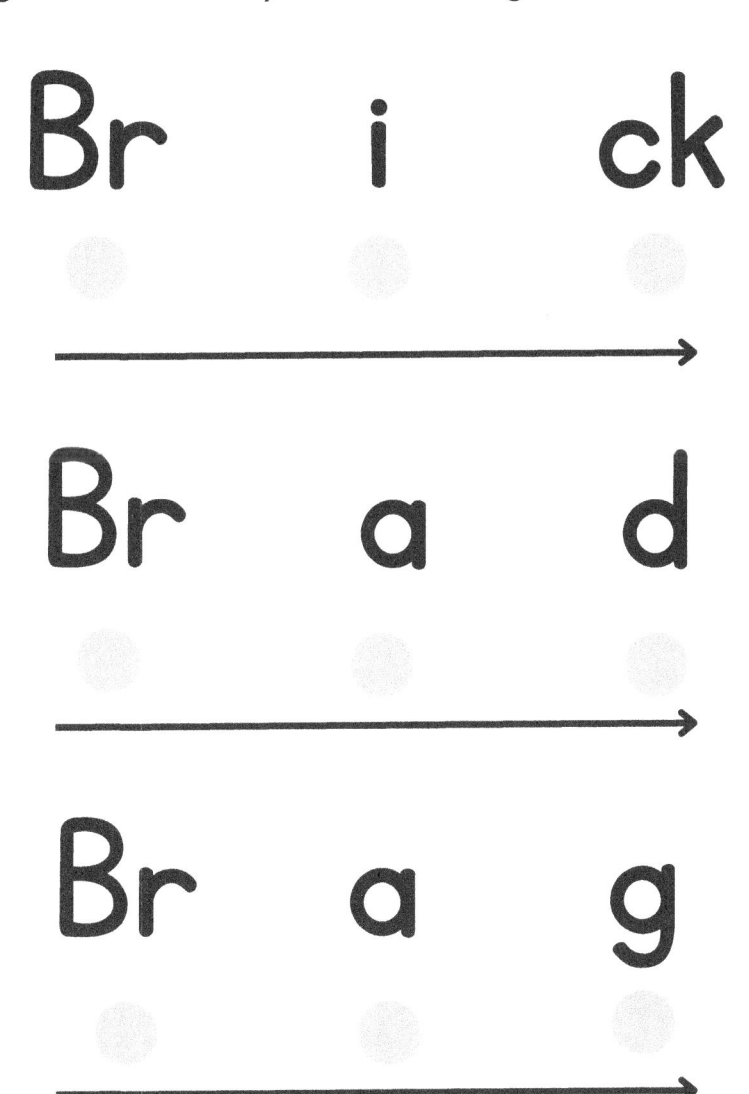

Br i ck

Br a d

Br a g

Tap it Out-2

Ask your student to use their finger to tap each circle below each letter of the word as they make it's sound. Then, blend each sound together while they slide their finger over the arrow.

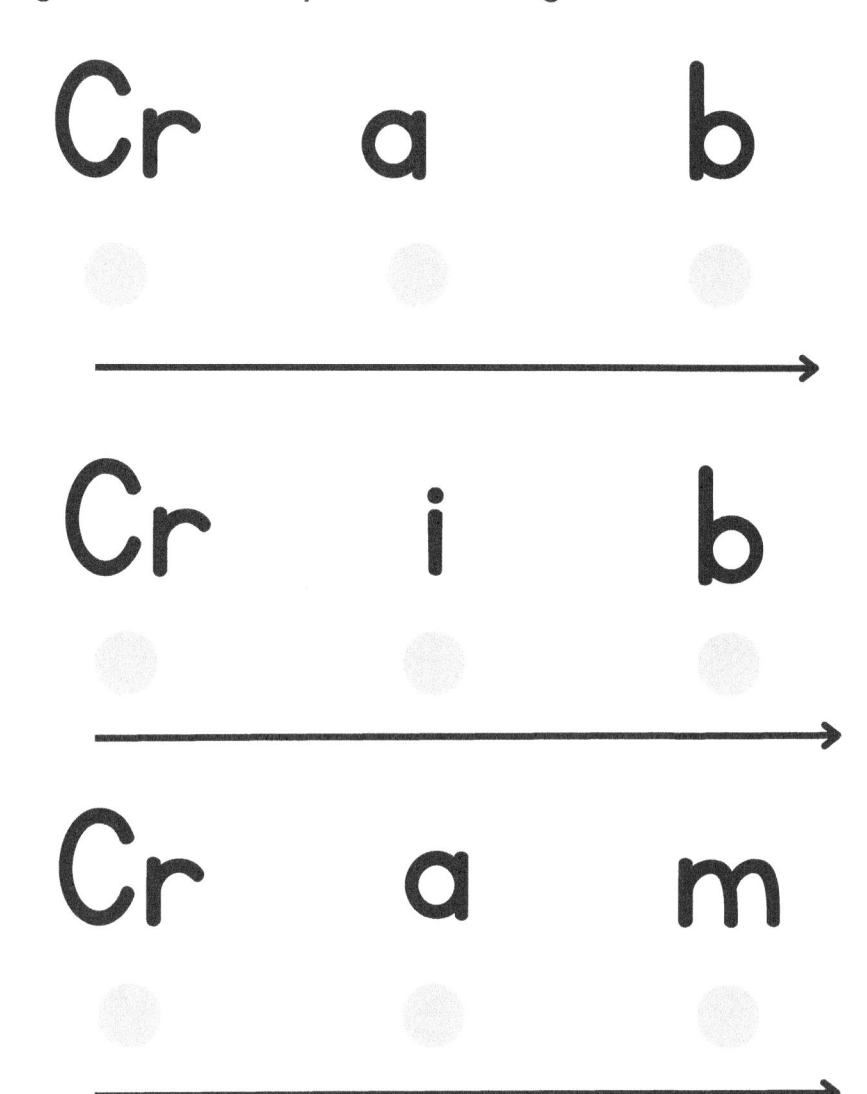

Cr a b

Cr i b

Cr a m

Read Read Read

Directions: Ask the student to read the following sentences.

The crab is on the sand.

Brad can bring the brick.

The is on the crib.

Directions: Ask the student to read the text and color the picture after they are done reading.

Brad sees a crab on the sand. The crab is crisp and big. It walks by a big rock. Brad brings a brush and hits the crab. The crab walks fast. Brad grins. The crab finds a crack and hid.

What's that Word?

Directions: Ask your child to write a letter to create a new word. After they write the letter, read the whole word aloud.

Cri __   Cra __

Br __ g   __ rop

C __ y   Bra __

Card Flip Fun!

Directions: Cut out the cards and place them face down. Take turns flipping the cards over saying the word within five seconds.

Crab   Brag

Bring   Brown

Cry   Craft

First to the Finish

Find a partner. Get a 6 sided die and two make-shift game pieces like a penny or a bead. Take turns rolling the die. Say the word you land on. The first to make it to the finish is the winner.

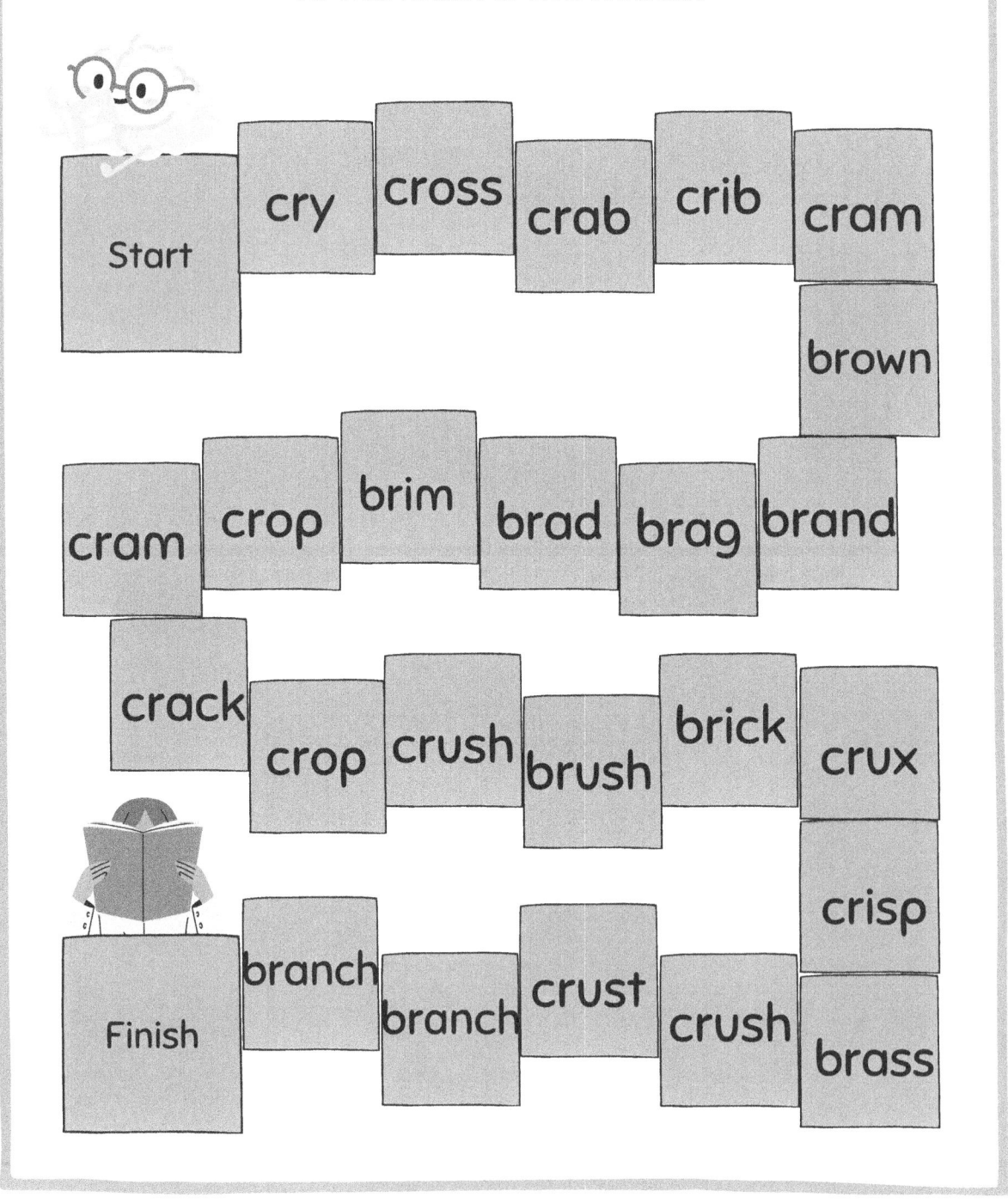

Start → cry → cross → crab → crib → cram → brown → brand → brag → brad → brim → crop → cram → crack → crop → crush → brush → brick → crux → crisp → brass → crush → crust → branch → branch → Finish

Name: Class:

SET 2
BLEND BR AND CR

Digraph Br, Cr Sounds

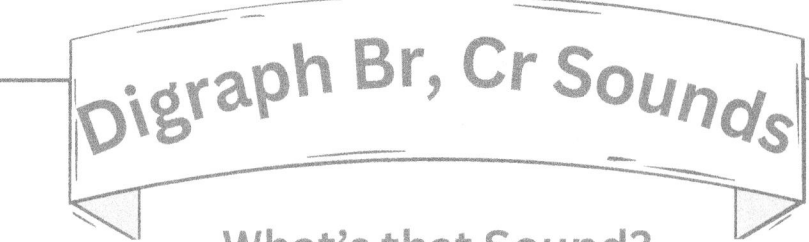

What's that Sound?

Ask your child to isolate the beginning, middle, or final sound in each word. Alternate each day and adjust the lesson to your student's needs. Do not allow them to see the words or the book while doing this exercise.

Crust   Brain

Crumb   Braid

Cruel   Brace

Blending Sounds

Directions: Ask your child to blend the following sounds into words. Do not show them the page.

Br-i-m   Cr-ow

Br-ay   Cr-a-b

Br-ea-d   Cr-o-p

Segmenting Sounds

Directions: Ask your child to break apart the following words into sounds. Do not show them the page.

Crate   Brick

Creek   Brisk

Crack   Bride

Tap it Out

Ask your student to use their finger to tap each circle below each letter of the word as they make it's sound. Then, blend each sound together while they slide their finger over the arrow.

Br a g

Br i m

Br a n

Tap it Out-2

Ask your student to use their finger to tap each circle below each letter of the word as they make it's sound. Then, blend each sound together while they slide their finger over the arrow.

Cr   o   p

Cr   i   b

Cr   a   ck

Read Read Read

Directions: Ask the student to read the following sentences.

The crop is crisp.

Brent will crush the can.

The crust is food.

Directions: Ask the student to read the text and color the picture after they are done reading.

The woman is in a dress. She will cross the big hall. Brent sees the woman and grins. The crab claps and brings her red crops. The woman brags. Both see a crib. The crab is glad.

What's that Word?

Directions: Ask your child to write a letter to create a new word. After they write the letter, read the whole word aloud.

Cro __   Cri __

Br __ sk   __ ru x

C __ ab   Bra __

Card Flip Fun!

Directions: Cut out the cards and place them face down. Take turns flipping the cards over saying the word within five seconds.

Crux	Woman
Crib	Brag
Crush	Brink

First to the Finish

Find a partner. Get a 6 sided die and two make-shift game pieces like a penny or a bead. Take turns rolling the die. Say the word you land on. The first to make it to the finish is the winner.

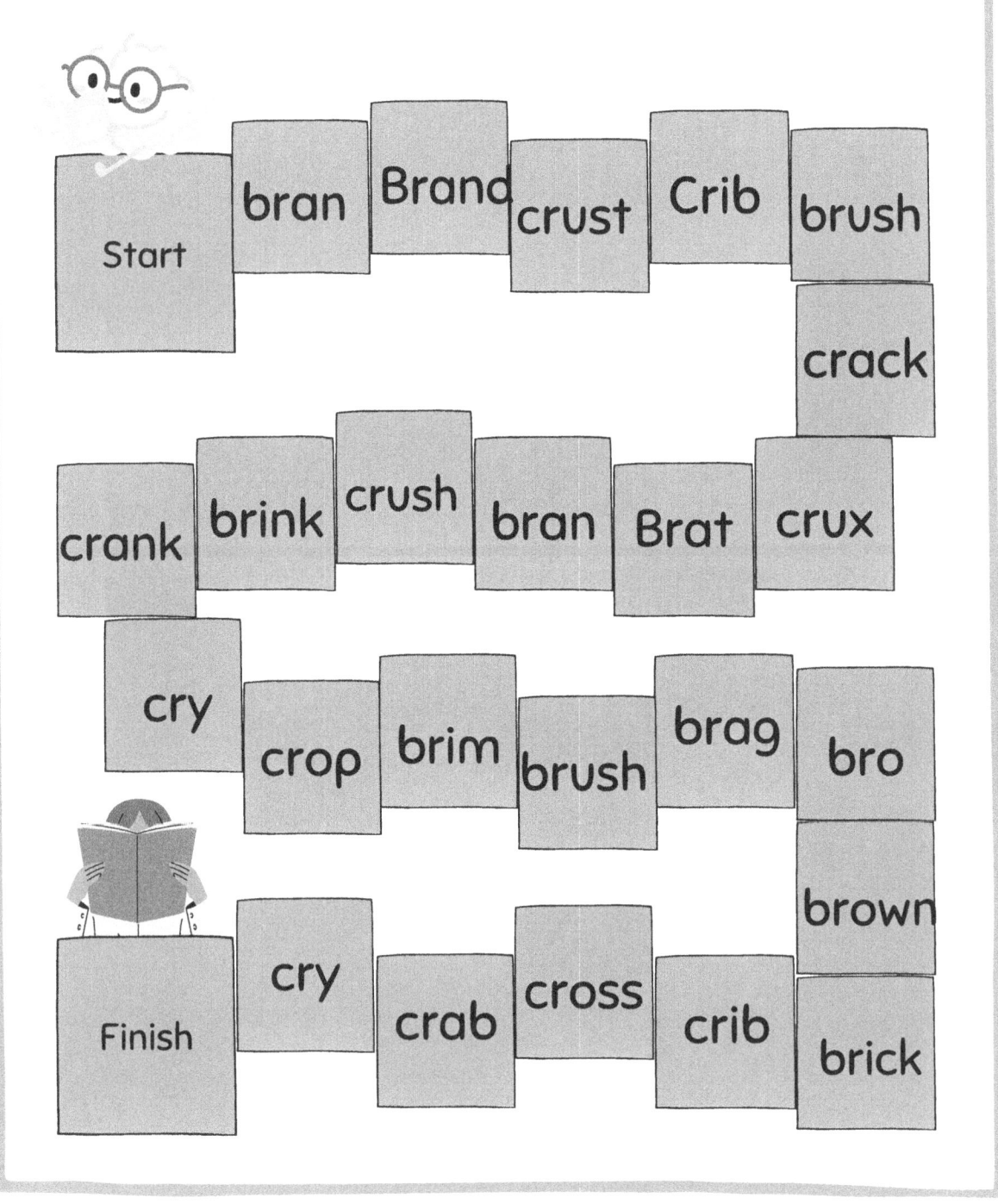

Start → bran → Brand → crust → Crib → brush → crack → crux → Brat → bran → crush → brink → crank → cry → crop → brim → brush → brag → bro → brown → brick → crib → cross → crab → cry → Finish

Name: _____ Class: _____

SET 1
BLEND DR AND FR

Digraph Dr, Fr Sounds

What's that Sound?

Ask your child to isolate the beginning, middle, or final sound in each word. Alternate each day and adjust the lesson to your student's needs. Do not allow them to see the words or the book while doing this exercise.

Dry	Fry
Drag	Frog
Drop	Fray

Blending Sounds

Directions: Ask your child to blend the following sounds into words. Do not show them the page.

Dr-i-p   Fr-y

Dr-i-ll   Fr-ay

Dr-a-g   Fr-ee

Segmenting Sounds

Directions: Ask your child to break apart the following words into sounds. Do not show them the page.

Fresh   Drop

Fret   Draw

Free   Drip

Tap it Out

Ask your student to use their finger to tap each circle below each letter of the word as they make it's sound. Then, blend each sound together while they slide their finger over the arrow.

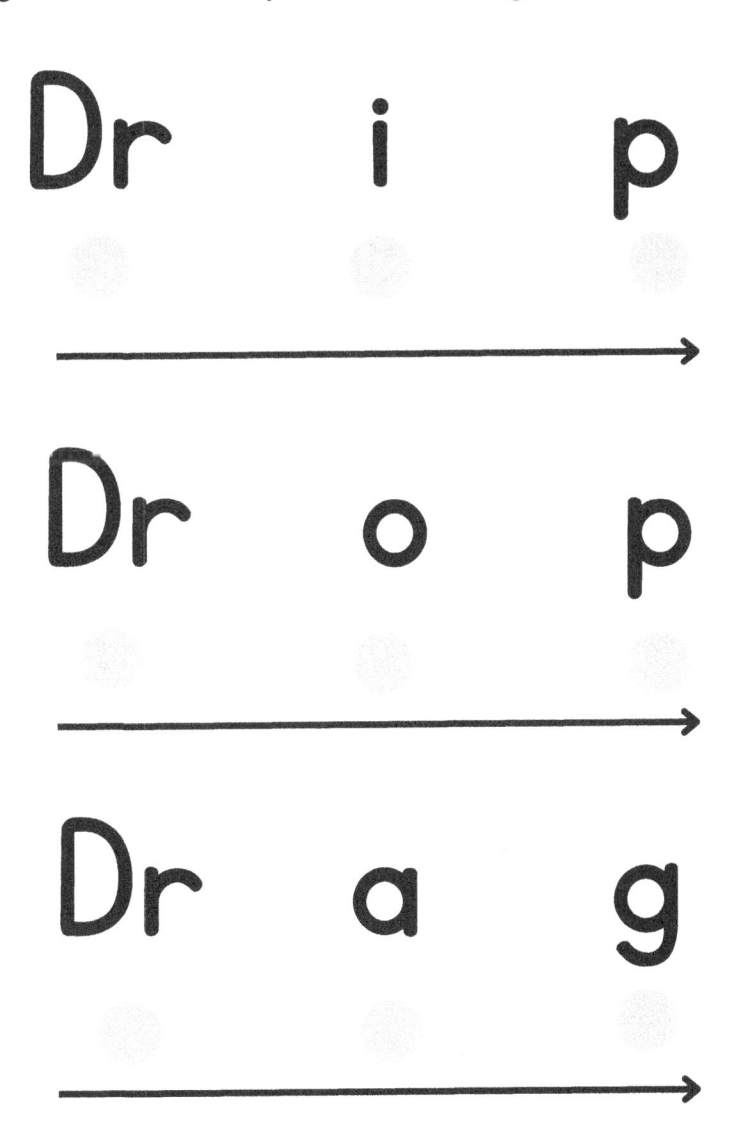

Dr   i   p

Dr   o   p

Dr   a   g

Tap it Out-2

Ask your student to use their finger to tap each circle below each letter of the word as they make it's sound. Then, blend each sound together while they slide their finger over the arrow.

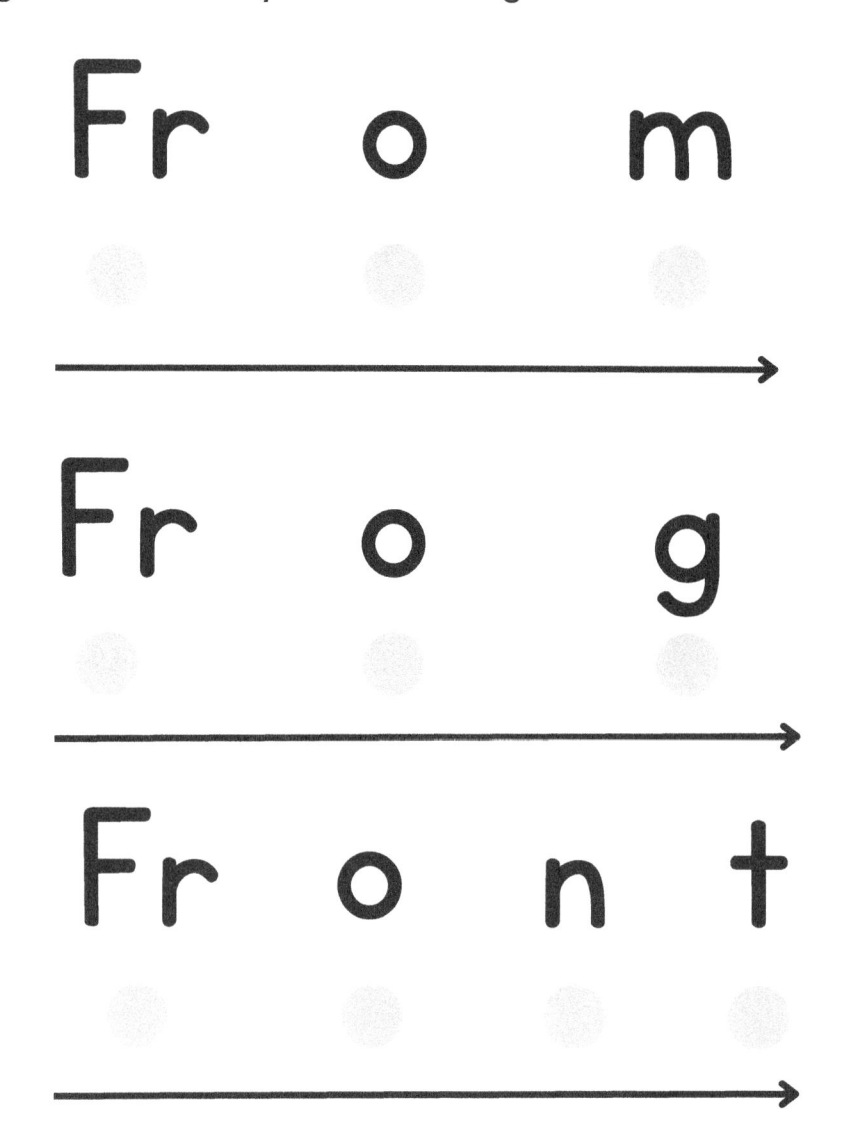

Fr o m

Fr o g

Fr o n t

Read
Read
Read

Directions: Ask the student to read the following sentences.

The frog will drink.

Fred can drop the drum.

The dress is fresh.

Directions: Ask the student to read the text and color the picture after they are done reading.

Bren has a red dress. The dress is dry and fresh. Bren will bring it to her room. She will grab a brush to brush it. Bren grins as she puts on the dress. The dress is a bit drab!

What's that Word?

Directions: Ask your child to write a letter to create a new word. After they write the letter, read the whole word aloud.

Dro __   Fr __

Fr __ m   __ ry

F __ og   Dri __

Card Flip Fun!

Directions: Cut out the cards and place them face down. Take turns flipping the cards over saying the word within five seconds.

Drip	Fresh
Drop	Fry
Drink	From

First to the Finish

Find a partner. Get a 6 sided die and two make-shift game pieces like a penny or a bead. Take turns rolling the die. Say the word you land on. The first to make it to the finish is the winner.

Start → dry → fry → from → drop → drip → drink → frog → drum → free → from → frat → fret → drank → fresh → dry → fry → dress → drill → draft → drink → drank → frozen → Frank → drop → Finish

Name: Class:

SET 2
BLEND DR AND FR

Digraph Dr, Fr Sounds

What's that Sound?

Ask your child to isolate the beginning, middle, or final sound in each word. Alternate each day and adjust the lesson to your student's needs. Do not allow them to see the words or the book while doing this exercise.

Dream   Free

Drain   Frisk

Drove   Frame

Blending Sounds

Directions: Ask your child to blend the following sounds into words. Do not show them the page.

Dr-a-g   Fr-ai-l

Dr-u-m   Fr-o-m

Dr-i-p   Fr-i-ll

Segmenting Sounds

Directions: Ask your child to break apart the following words into sounds. Do not show them the page.

Drink   Frown

Drape   Front

Draft   Froze

Tap it Out

Ask your student to use their finger to tap each circle below each letter of the word as they make it's sound. Then, blend each sound together while they slide their finger over the arrow.

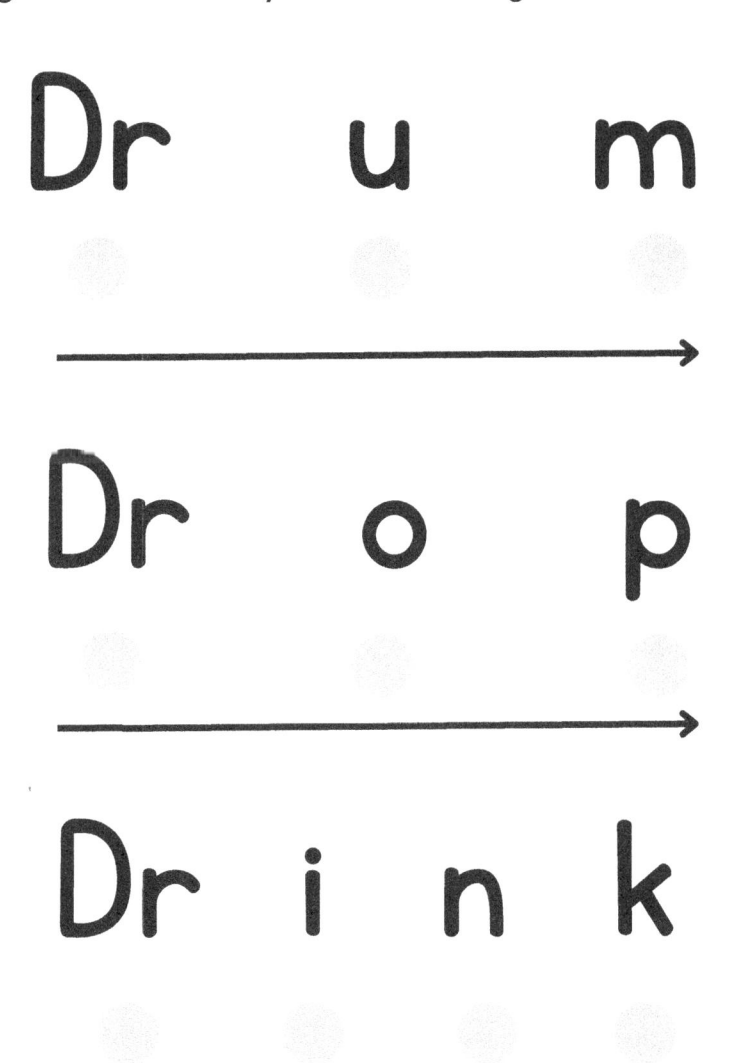

Dr   u   m

⟶

Dr   o   p

⟶

Dr   i   n   k

⟶

Tap it Out -2

Ask your student to use their finger to tap each circle below each letter of the word as they make it's sound. Then, blend each sound together while they slide their finger over the arrow.

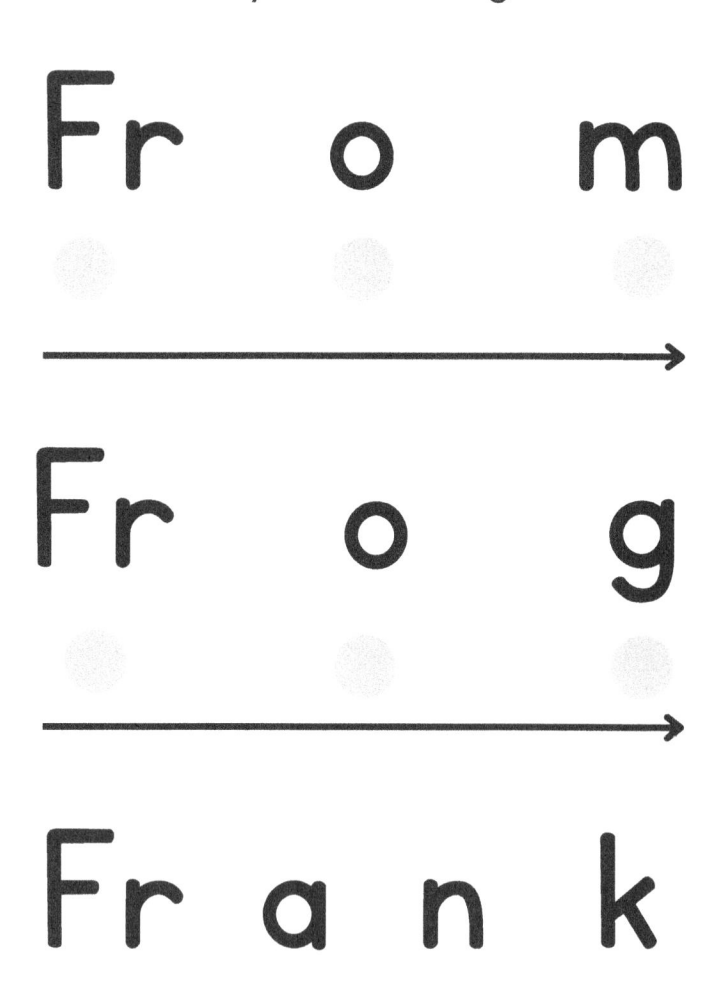

Fr o m

Fr o g

Fr a n k

Read
Read
Read

Directions: Ask the student to read the following sentences.

The frog is in the pond.

Frank will drag the sled.

Fran will fry fish.

Directions: Ask the student to read the text and color the picture after they are done reading.

Frank sees a frog by the drum. The frog is fresh. It will drag frost as it walks. Frank brings a small branch to the frog. The frog will grab the branch to the front. Frank will bring a drink to the frog. The frog will drink it.

What's that Word?

Directions: Ask your child to write a letter to create a new word. After they write the letter, read the whole word aloud.

Dru __   Dr __

Fr __ sh   __ rip

D __ ag   Dro __

Card Flip Fun!

Directions: Cut out the cards and place them face down. Take turns flipping the cards over saying the word within five seconds.

From	Drink
Frost	Drop
Front	Dry

First to the Finish

Find a partner. Get a 6 sided die and two make-shift game pieces like a penny or a bead. Take turns rolling the die. Say the word you land on. The first to make it to the finish is the winner.

Start → drill → frill → fry → dry → from → drag → drum → free → from → frat → fret → drop → dress → Frank → frog → frisk → drank → drink → drum → front → from → free → frizz → fresh → Finish

Name: Class:

SET 1
BLEND GR, TR, PR

Digraph Gr, Tr, Pr, Sounds

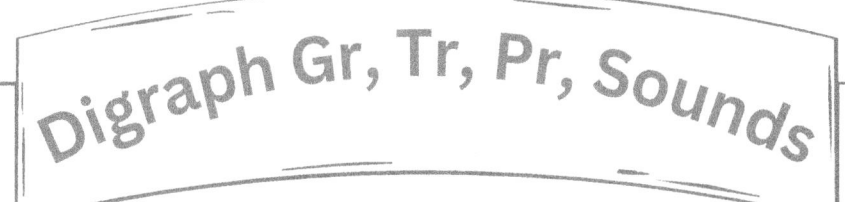

What's that Sound?

Ask your child to isolate the beginning, middle, or final sound in each word. Alternate each day and adjust the lesson to your student's needs. Do not allow them to see the words or the book while doing this exercise.

Grab   Tree

Grad   Pry

Try   Pray

Blending Sounds

Directions: Ask your child to blend the following sounds into words. Do not show them the page.

Gr-ow   Gr-i-d

Tr-y   Tr-i-m

Pr-y   Pr-e-y

Segmenting Sounds

Directions: Ask your child to break apart the following words into sounds. Do not show them the page.

Grab   Tree

Grin   Prop

Trim   Prep

Tap it Out

Ask your student to use their finger to tap each circle below each letter of the word as they make it's sound. Then, blend each sound together while they slide their finger over the arrow.

Gr i d

Gr a b

Tr i p

Tap it Out -2

Ask your student to use their finger to tap each circle below each letter of the word as they make it's sound. Then, blend each sound together while they slide their finger over the arrow.

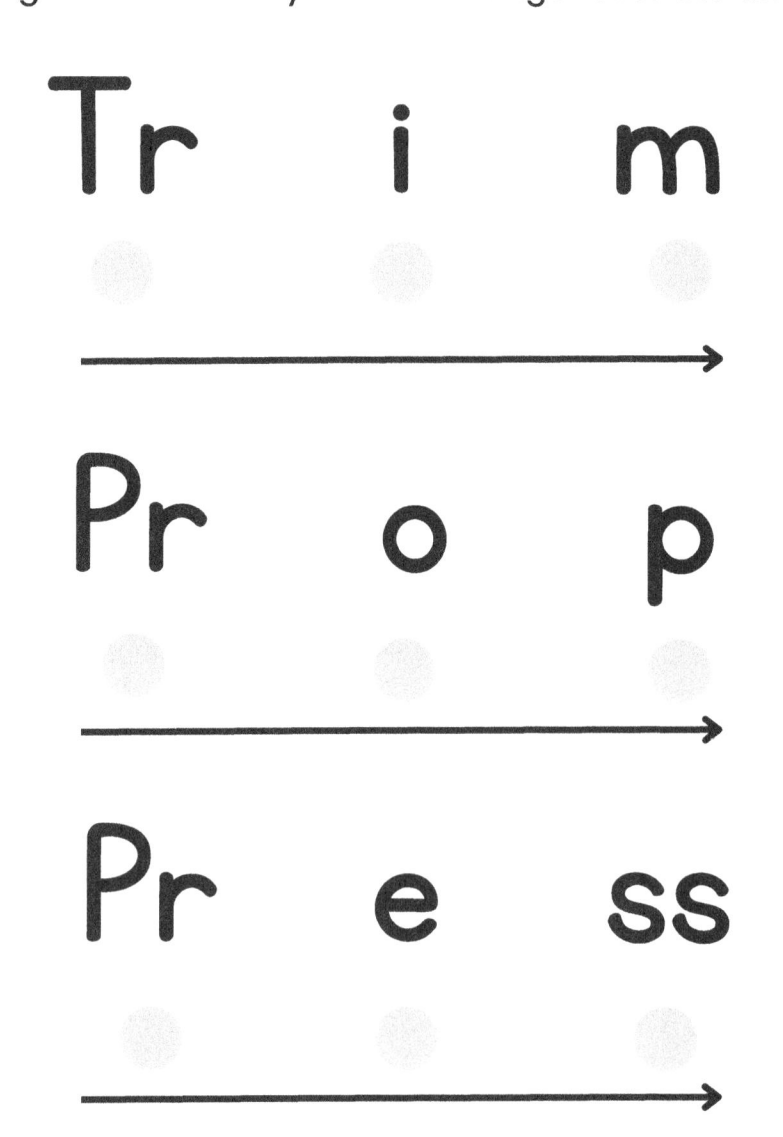

Tr i m

Pr o p

Pr e ss

Read
Read
Read

Directions: Ask the student to read the following sentences.

The trip is a trap.

Pam will grab the print.

The frog will trip.

Directions: Ask the student to read the text and color the picture after they are done reading.

Grant spots a grub in the trap. The grub is trim and slim. He will pry the grub and put it on a big track. The grub must trust Grant. Grant grins as the grub rests.

What's that Word?

Directions: Ask your child to write a letter to create a new word. After they write the letter, read the whole word aloud.

Gri __   Tr __

Tr __ st   __ ry

G __ am   Tra __

Card Flip Fun!

Directions: Cut out the cards and place them face down. Take turns flipping the cards over saying the word within five seconds.

Grass	Grub
Grill	Trash
Prank	Trip

First to the Finish

Find a partner. Get a 6 sided die and two make-shift game pieces like a penny or a bead. Take turns rolling the die. Say the word you land on. The first to make it to the finish is the winner.

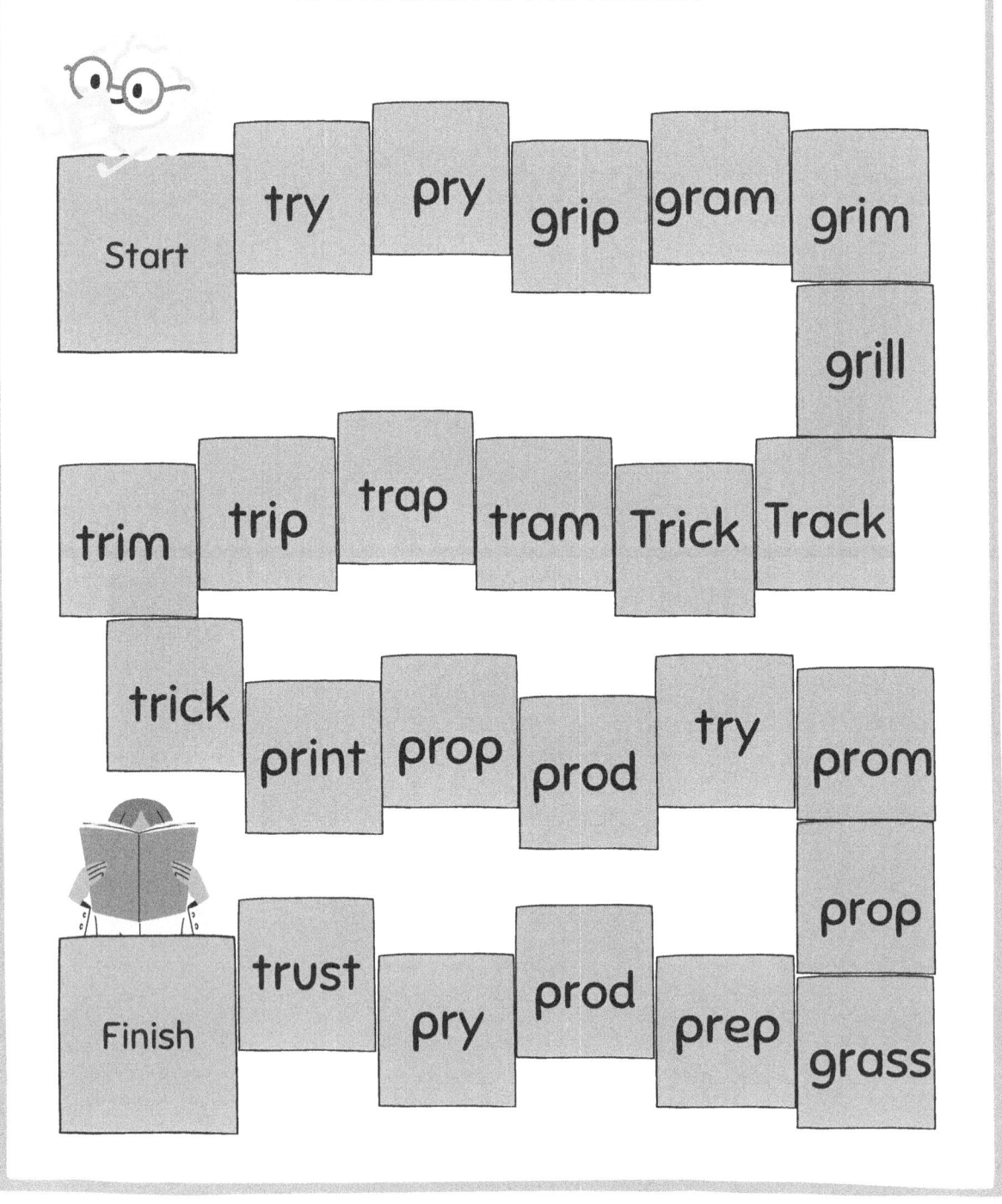

Start → try → pry → grip → gram → grim → grill → Track → Trick → tram → trap → trip → trim → trick → print → prop → prod → try → prom → prop → grass → prep → prod → pry → trust → Finish

Name: Class:

SET 2
BLEND GR, TR, PR

Digraph Gr, Tr, Pr, Sounds

What's that Sound?

Ask your child to isolate the beginning, middle, or final sound in each word. Alternate each day and adjust the lesson to your student's needs. Do not allow them to see the words or the book while doing this exercise.

Grand   Tray

Grill   Prom

Trap   Prod

Blending Sounds

Directions: Ask your child to blend the following sounds into words. Do not show them the page.

Pr-e-p   Gr-ey

Pr-o-m   Tr-ue

Gr-i-d   Tr-i-o

Segmenting Sounds

Directions: Ask your child to break apart the following words into sounds. Do not show them the page.

Trio   Grip

Trey   Prod

Grew   Press

Tap it Out

Ask your student to use their finger to tap each circle below each letter of the word as they make it's sound. Then, blend each sound together while they slide their finger over the arrow.

Gr i m

Gr i d

Tr e ck

Tap it Out -2

Ask your student to use their finger to tap each circle below each letter of the word as they make it's sound. Then, blend each sound together while they slide their finger over the arrow.

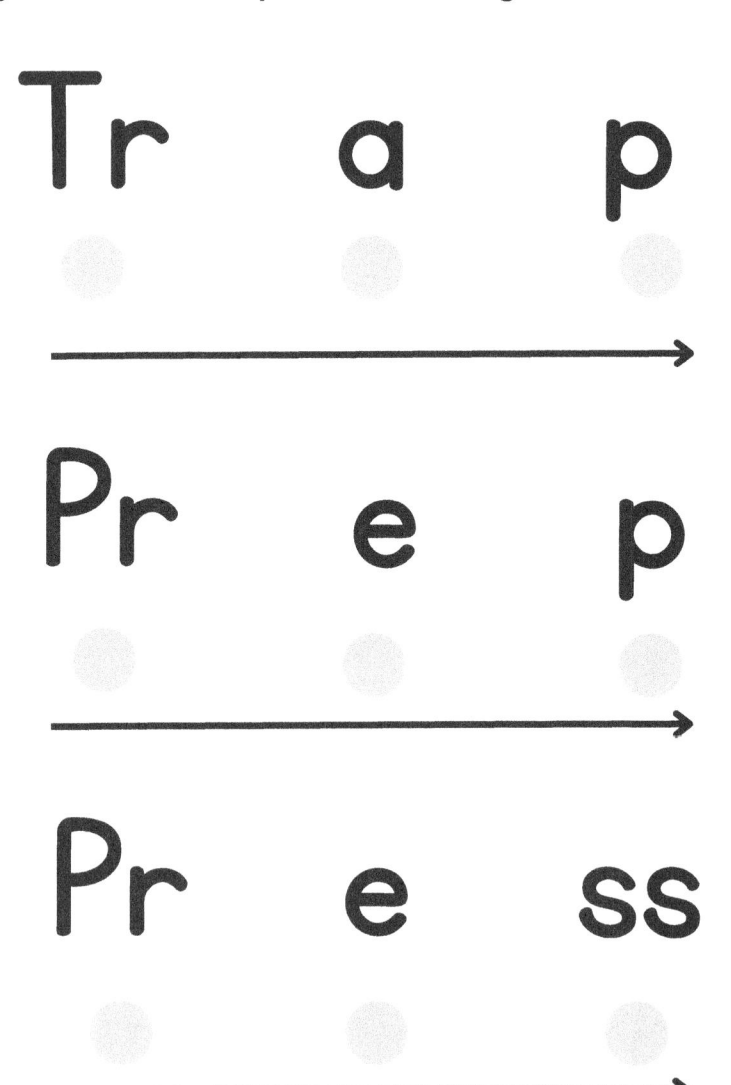

Tr a p

Pr e p

Pr e ss

Read
Read
Read

Directions: Ask the student to read the following sentences.

The truck went up.

I will press the button.

Gran has a red dress.

Directions: Ask the student to read the text and color the picture after they are done reading.

Tron can see a tree in the grass. The tree is big and trim. Tron will grab a small prop and press it in the tree. The trunk of the tree gets big. Tron grins and claps. The tree is grand!

What's that Word?

Directions: Ask your child to write a letter to create a new word. After they write the letter, read the whole word aloud.

Gra __   Pr __

Tr __ p   __ ram

G __ ill   Tra __

Card Flip Fun!

Directions: Cut out the cards and place them face down. Take turns flipping the cards over saying the word within five seconds.

Truck	Poxy
Trap	Gruff
Pry	Grill

First to the Finish

Find a partner. Get a 6 sided die and two make-shift game pieces like a penny or a bead. Take turns rolling the die. Say the word you land on. The first to make it to the finish is the winner.

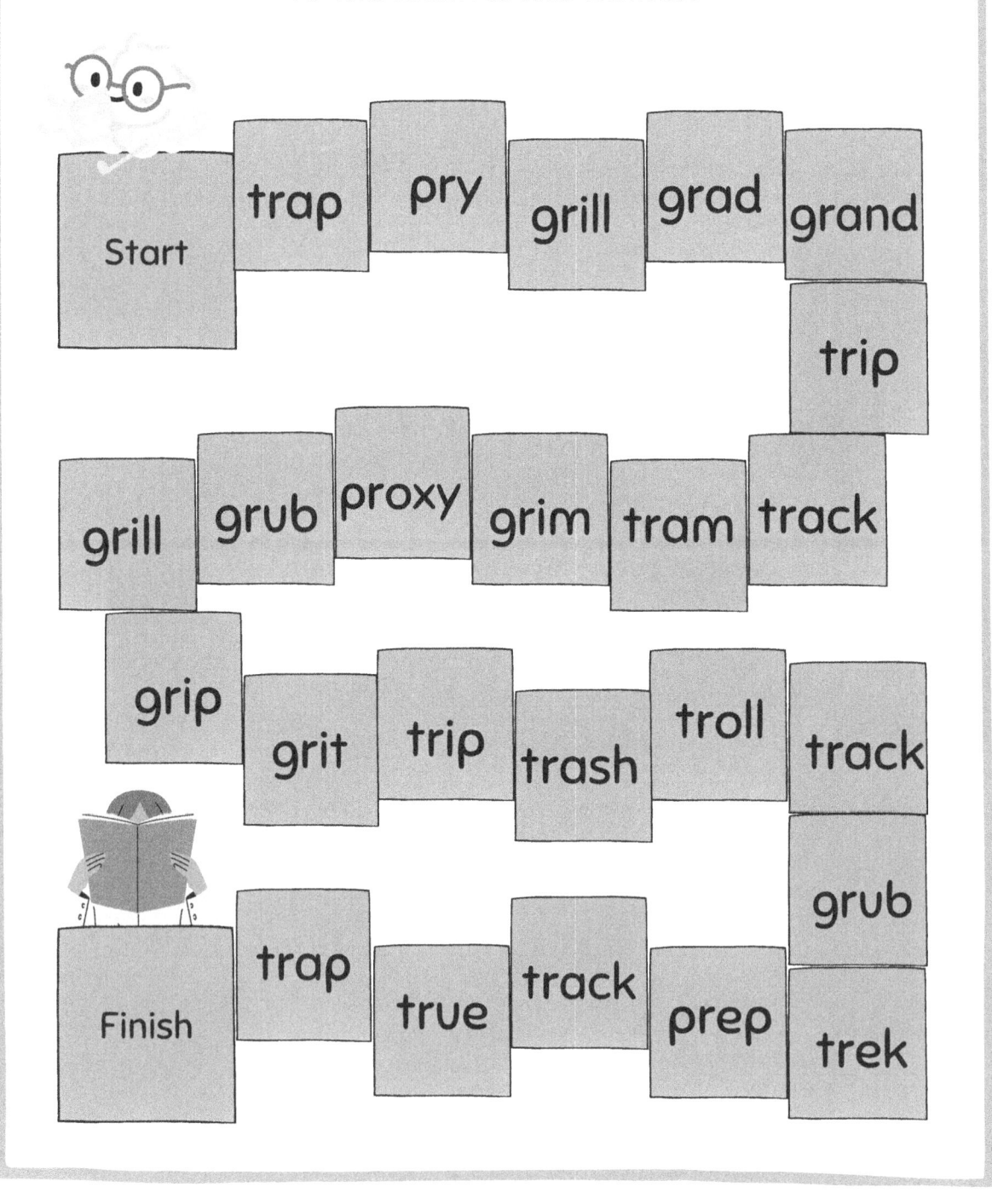

Start → trap → pry → grill → grad → grand → trip → track → tram → grim → proxy → grub → grill → grip → grit → trip → trash → troll → track → grub → trek → prep → track → true → trap → Finish

Name: Class:

SET 3
BLEND GR, TR, PR

Digraph Gr, Tr, Pr, Sounds

What's that Sound?

Ask your child to isolate the beginning, middle, or final sound in each word. Alternate each day and adjust the lesson to your student's needs. Do not allow them to see the words or the book while doing this exercise.

Greed   Track

Growl   Prize

Tread   Praise

Blending Sounds

Directions: Ask your child to blend the following sounds into words. Do not show them the page.

Pr-i-ce   Gr-i-ll

Pr-i-m   Tr-a-m

Gr-i-n   Tr-oy

Segmenting Sounds

Directions: Ask your child to break apart the following words into sounds. Do not show them the page.

Green   Prowl

Growl   Track

Prime   Train

Tap it Out

Ask your student to use their finger to tap each circle below each letter of the word as they make it's sound. Then, blend each sound together while they slide their finger over the arrow.

Gr i p

Gr a ss

Tr e n d

Tap it Out -2

Ask your student to use their finger to tap each circle below each letter of the word as they make it's sound. Then, blend each sound together while they slide their finger over the arrow.

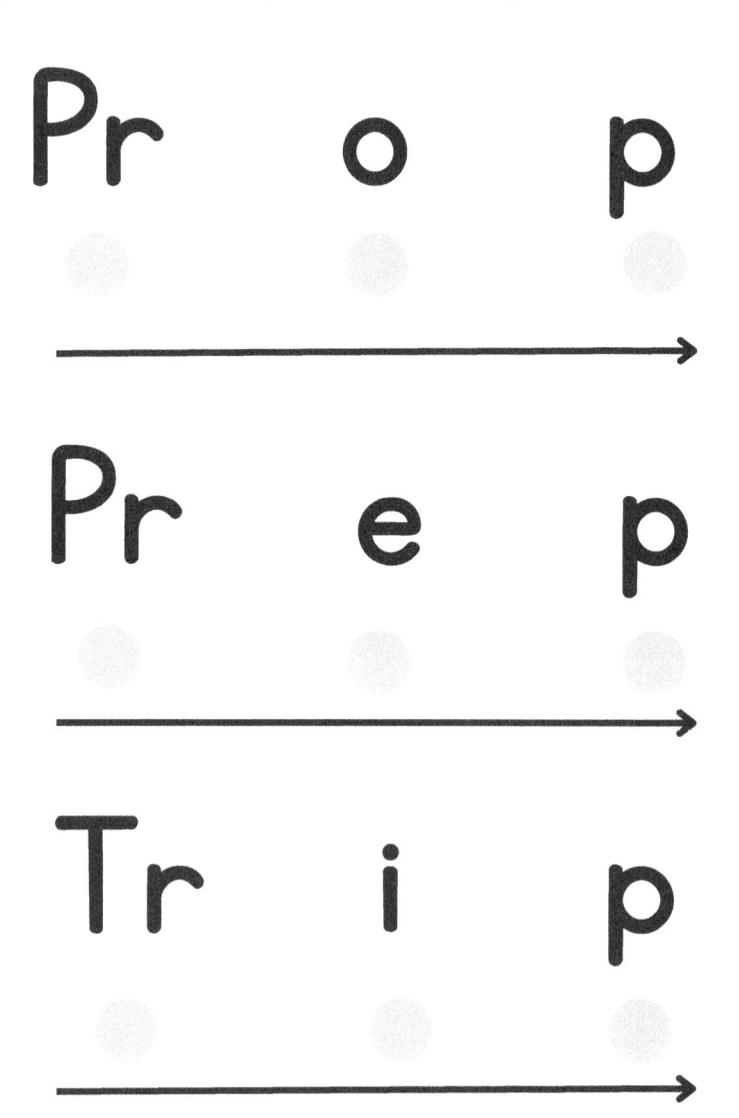

Pr   o   p

Pr   e   p

Tr   i   p

Read Read Read

Directions: Ask the student to read the following sentences.

The press will trip.

Greg will pry the lid.

The grass is wet.

Directions: Ask the student to read the text and color the picture after they are done reading.

The train is on the track. Greg will press the red button. The train trips and then drifts. Grant grabs his hat as the train goes fast. The train stops at a tree. Greg and Grant grin and clap.

What's that Word?

Directions: Ask your child to write a letter to create a new word. After they write the letter, read the whole word aloud.

Pri __   Tr __

Tr __ m   __ rap

G __ am   Tre __

Card Flip Fun!

Directions: Cut out the cards and place them face down. Take turns flipping the cards over saying the word within five seconds.

Trick		Grim

Train		Try

Press		Prep

First to the Finish

Find a partner. Get a 6 sided die and two make-shift game pieces like a penny or a bead. Take turns rolling the die. Say the word you land on. The first to make it to the finish is the winner.

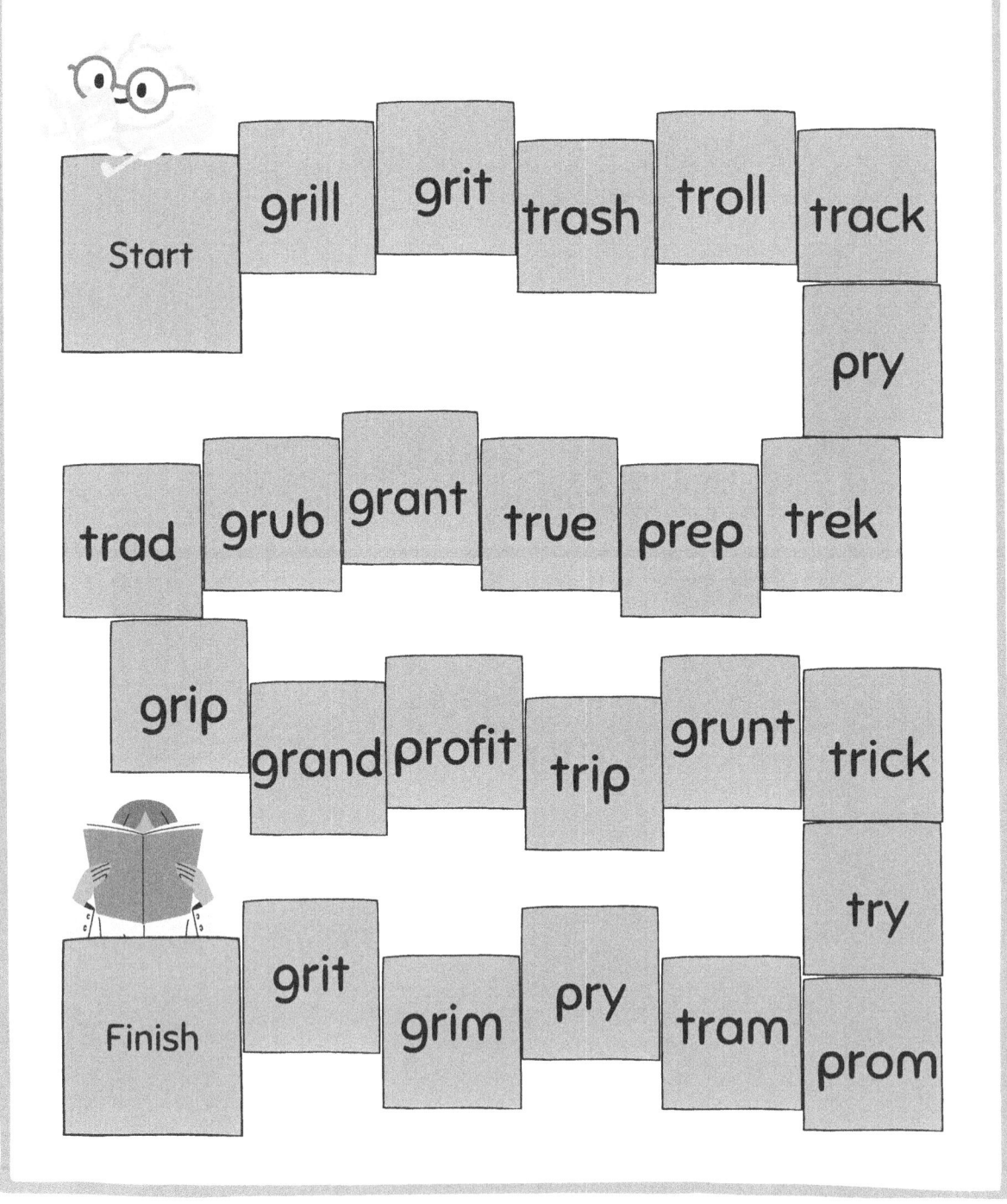

Start → grill → grit → trash → troll → track → pry → trek → prep → true → grant → grub → trad → grip → grand → profit → trip → grunt → trick → try → prom → tram → pry → grim → grit → Finish

Name: Class:

SET 1
BLEND SC AND SK

Digraph Sc and Sk Sounds

What's that Sound?

Ask your child to isolate the beginning, middle, or final sound in each word. Alternate each day and adjust the lesson to your student's needs. Do not allow them to see the words or the book while doing this exercise.

Scar Skate

Scam Sky

Scan Skill

Blending Sounds

Directions: Ask your child to blend the following sounds into words. Do not show them the page.

Sc-ar   Sk-i

Sc-a-m   Sk-y

Sc-o-tt   Sk-i-m

Segmenting Sounds

Directions: Ask your child to break apart the following words into sounds. Do not show them the page.

Skunk   Skill

Skulk   Scary

Skull   Scoff

Tap it Out

Ask your student to use their finger to tap each circle below each letter of the word as they make it's sound. Then, blend each sound together while they slide their finger over the arrow.

Sk   i

Sk   i   m

Sk   i   p

Tap it Out -2

Ask your student to use their finger to tap each circle below each letter of the word as they make it's sound. Then, blend each sound together while they slide their finger over the arrow.

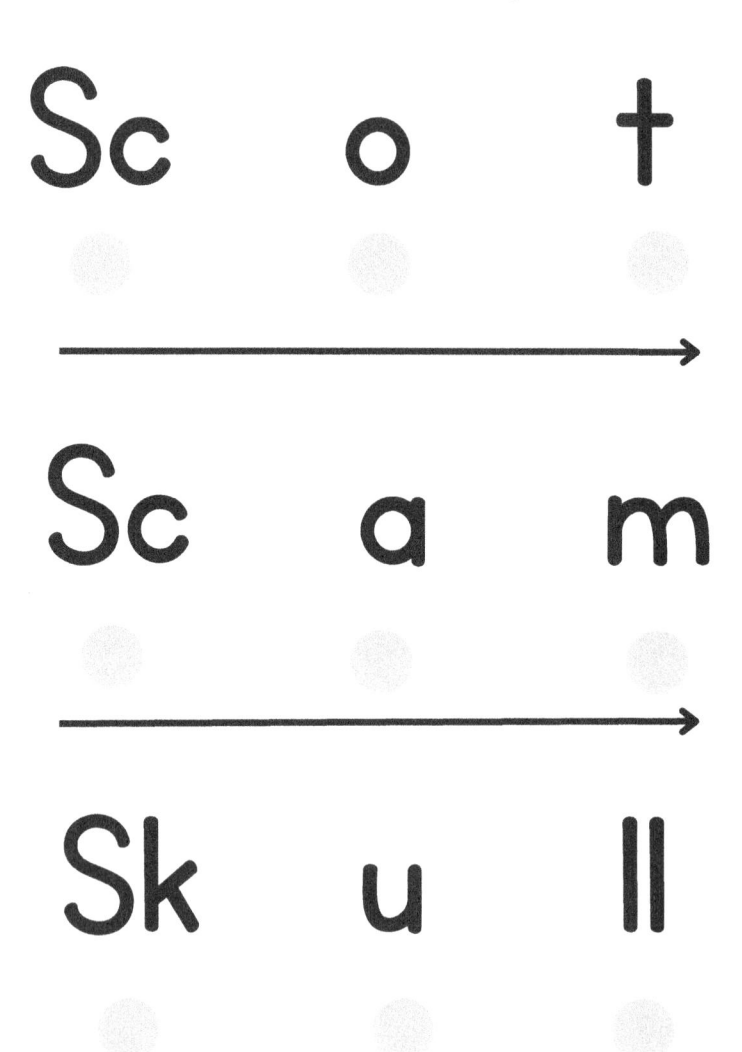

Sc   o   t

Sc   a   m

Sk   u   ll

Read
Read
Read

Directions: Ask the student to read the following sentences.

The skunk ran fast.

Skip will scan the map.

The sketch is scum.

Directions: Ask the student to read the text and color the picture after they are done reading.

The scarf is red and soft. Skip will grab the scarf. He will scan the tag. The scarf slips and drops. Skip picks it up and grins. He will fold the scarf and stack it. The scarf is Scotch.

What's that Word?

Directions: Ask your child to write a letter to create a new word. After they write the letter, read the whole word aloud.

Ski __   Sk __

Sk __ m   __ can

S __ i   Sco __

Card Flip Fun!

Directions: Cut out the cards and place them face down. Take turns flipping the cards over saying the word within five seconds.

Skill	Scan
Sky	Ski
Scum	Skim

First to the Finish

Find a partner. Get a 6 sided die and two make-shift game pieces like a penny or a bead. Take turns rolling the die. Say the word you land on. The first to make it to the finish is the winner.

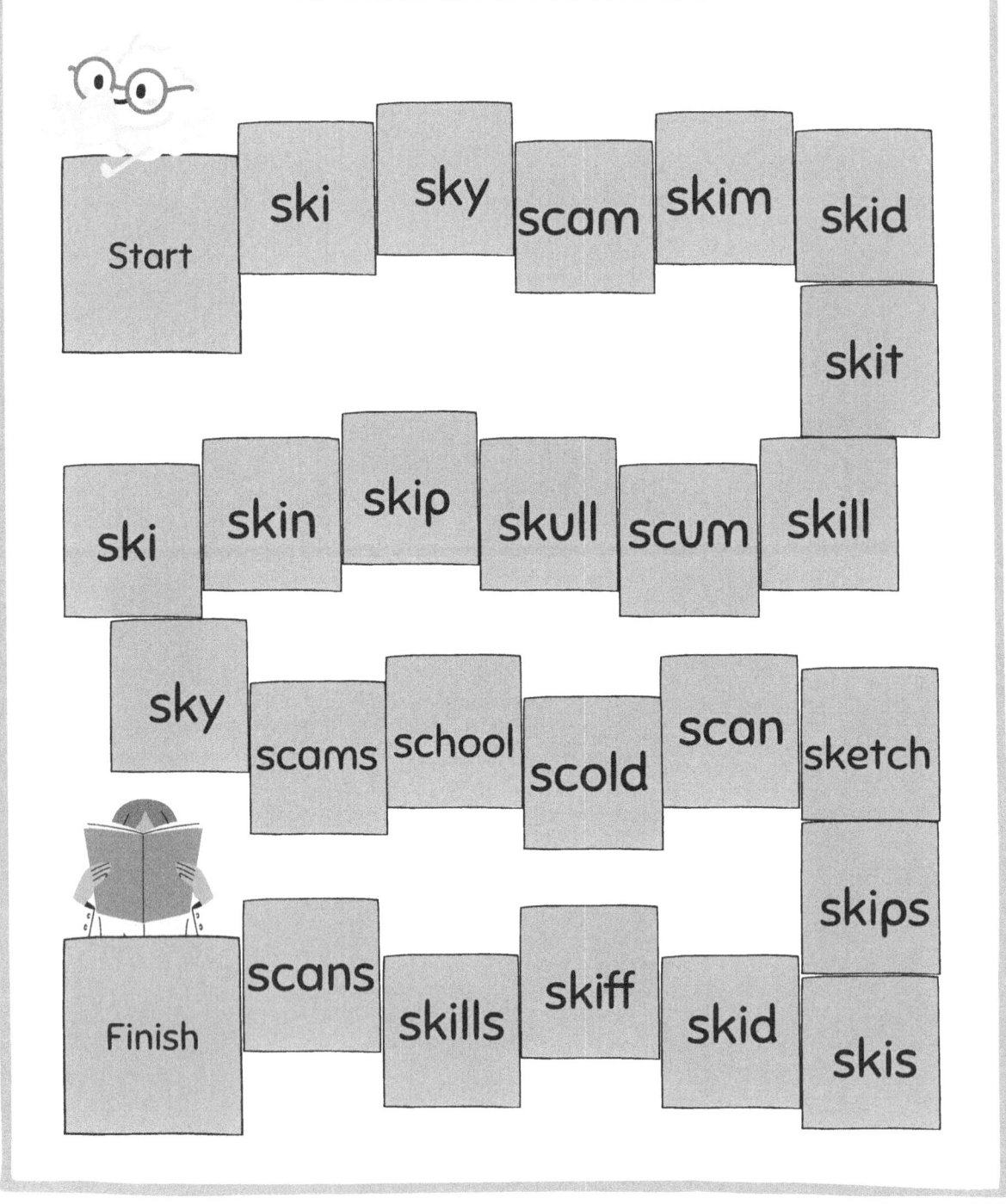

Start → ski → sky → scam → skim → skid → skit → skill → scum → skull → skip → skin → ski → sky → scams → school → scold → scan → sketch → skips → skis → skid → skiff → skills → scans → Finish

Name: _____ Class: _____

SET 2
BLEND SC AND SK

Digraph Sc and Sk Sounds

What's that Sound?

Ask your child to isolate the beginning, middle, or final sound in each word. Alternate each day and adjust the lesson to your student's needs. Do not allow them to see the words or the book while doing this exercise.

Sky	Scale
Skirt	Skill
Skies	Scout

Blending Sounds

Directions: Ask your child to blend the following sounds into words. Do not show them the page.

Sc-a-n   Sk-i-t

Sk-i-p   Sk-i-ll

Sc-ar   Sk-i-n

Segmenting Sounds

Directions: Ask your child to break apart the following words into sounds. Do not show them the page.

Scam	Skate

Scoop	Skill

Score	Skid

Tap it Out

Ask your student to use their finger to tap each circle below each letter of the word as they make it's sound. Then, blend each sound together while they slide their finger over the arrow.

Sk   y

Sk   i   n

Sk   i   t

Tap it Out -2

Ask your student to use their finger to tap each circle below each letter of the word as they make it's sound. Then, blend each sound together while they slide their finger over the arrow.

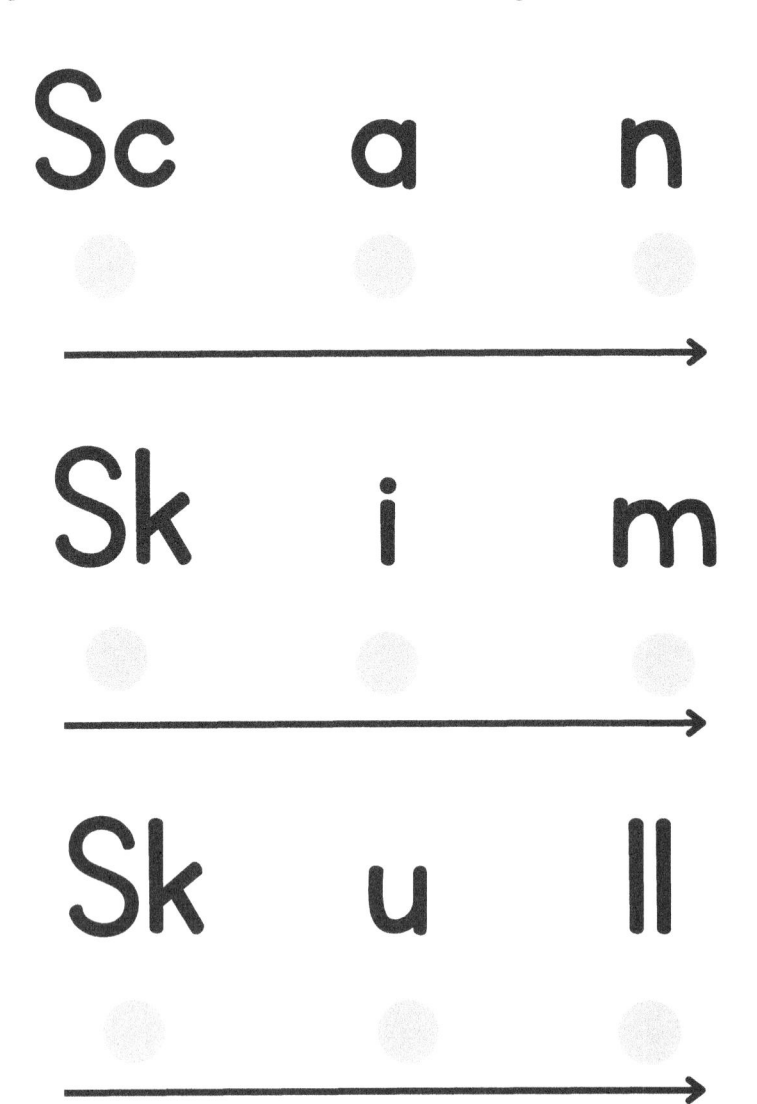

Sc a n

Sk i m

Sk u ll

Read
Read
Read

Directions: Ask the student to read the following sentences.

Scan the small skull.

The skit was fun.

The skunk will skip by.

Directions: Ask the student to read the text and color the picture after they are done reading.

Scan the sky for skunks. The sky is big. Skip looks up at the sky. He will scan the sky with skill. A small bug will skim by. Skip will skip and grin. The sky has scum. But Skip will scan the sky with skill.

What's that Word?

Directions: Ask your child to write a letter to create a new word.
After they write the letter, read the whole word aloud.

Ski __		Sk __ p

Sc __ n		__ cam

S __ in		Ski __

Card Flip Fun!

Directions: Cut out the cards and place them face down. Take turns flipping the cards over saying the word within five seconds.

Skill	Skip
Scan	Sky
Skit	Skim

First to the Finish

Find a partner. Get a 6 sided die and two make-shift game pieces like a penny or a bead. Take turns rolling the die. Say the word you land on. The first to make it to the finish is the winner.

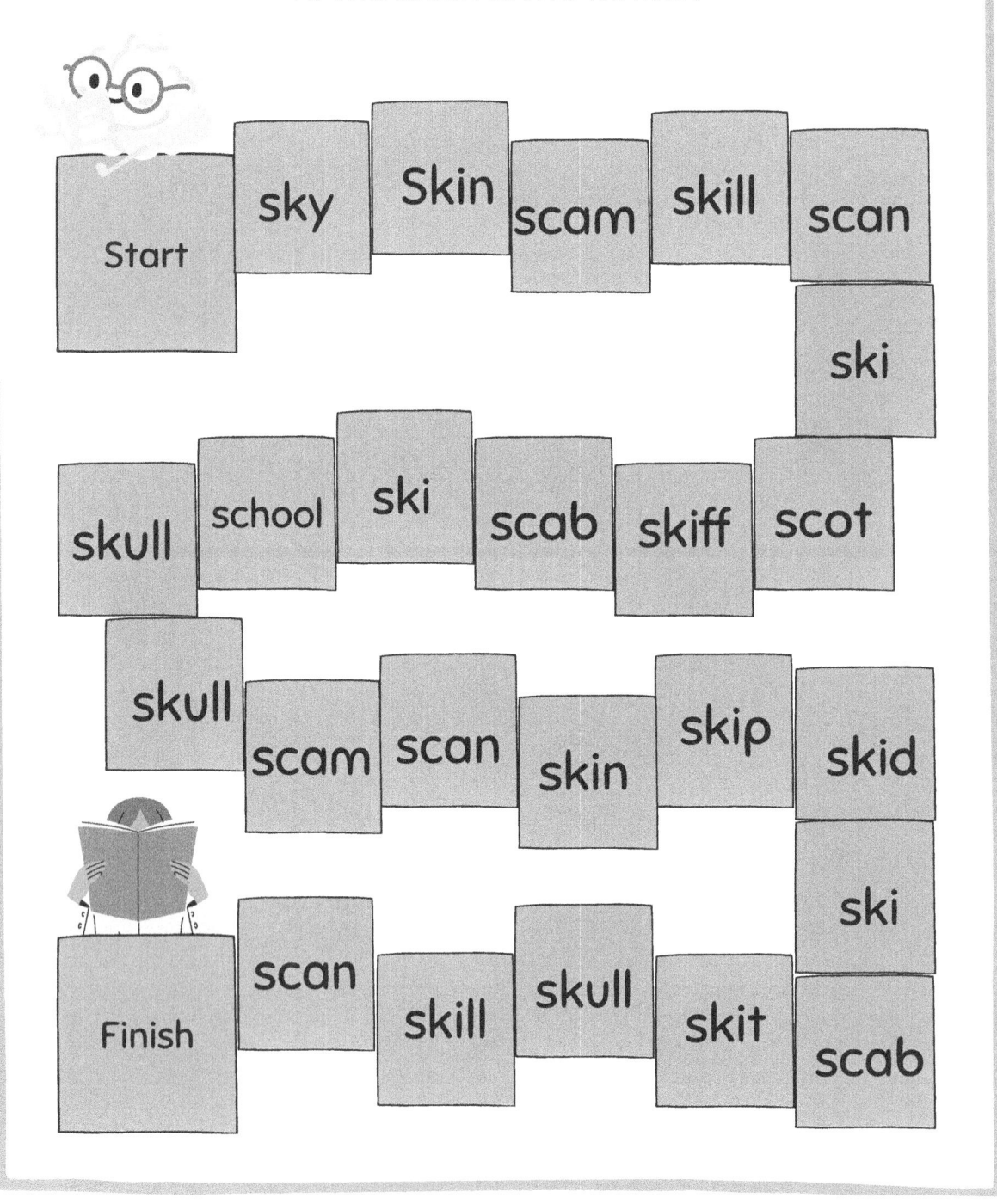

Start → sky → Skin → scam → skill → scan → ski → scot → skiff → scab → ski → school → skull → skull → scam → scan → skin → skip → skid → ski → scab → skit → skull → skill → scan → Finish

Name: Class:

SET 1
BLEND SN AND SM

Digraph Sn and Sm Sounds

What's that Sound?

Ask your child to isolate the beginning, middle, or final sound in each word. Alternate each day and adjust the lesson to your student's needs. Do not allow them to see the words or the book while doing this exercise.

Snap   Smug

Snow   Small

Snug   Smell

Blending Sounds

Directions: Ask your child to blend the following sounds into words. Do not show them the page.

Sn-u-g   Sm-a-ll

Sn-ai-l   Sm-e-ll

Sn-i-ff   Sm-u-g

Segmenting Sounds

Directions: Ask your child to break apart the following words into sounds. Do not show them the page.

Snarl   Smoke

Snore   Small

Snort   Smell

Tap it Out

Ask your student to use their finger to tap each circle below each letter of the word as they make it's sound. Then, blend each sound together while they slide their finger over the arrow.

Sn a ck s

Sn u g

Sn i p

Tap it Out -2

Ask your student to use their finger to tap each circle below each letter of the word as they make it's sound. Then, blend each sound together while they slide their finger over the arrow.

Sm u g

Sm a sh

Sm e ll

Read
Read
Read

Directions: Ask the student to read the following sentences.

The snack is small.

Smith will smell the smog.

The smock will snap.

Directions: Ask the student to read the text and color the picture after they are done reading.

The snail has a smell. It is snug in the smog. A snail can snap quick. Can you snatch it? Smith is smitten. But the snail runs quick. It will not smush if you smash it. Smith wants it. But the snail is quick.

What's that Word?

Directions: Ask your child to write a letter to create a new word. After they write the letter, read the whole word aloud.

Sna__e   Sn__p

Sm__g   __niff

S__ug   Smel__

Card Flip Fun!

Directions: Cut out the cards and place them face down. Take turns flipping the cards over saying the word within five seconds.

Snip	Sniff
Snack	Smug
Snail	Smell

First to the Finish

Find a partner. Get a 6 sided die and two make-shift game pieces like a penny or a bead. Take turns rolling the die. Say the word you land on. The first to make it to the finish is the winner.

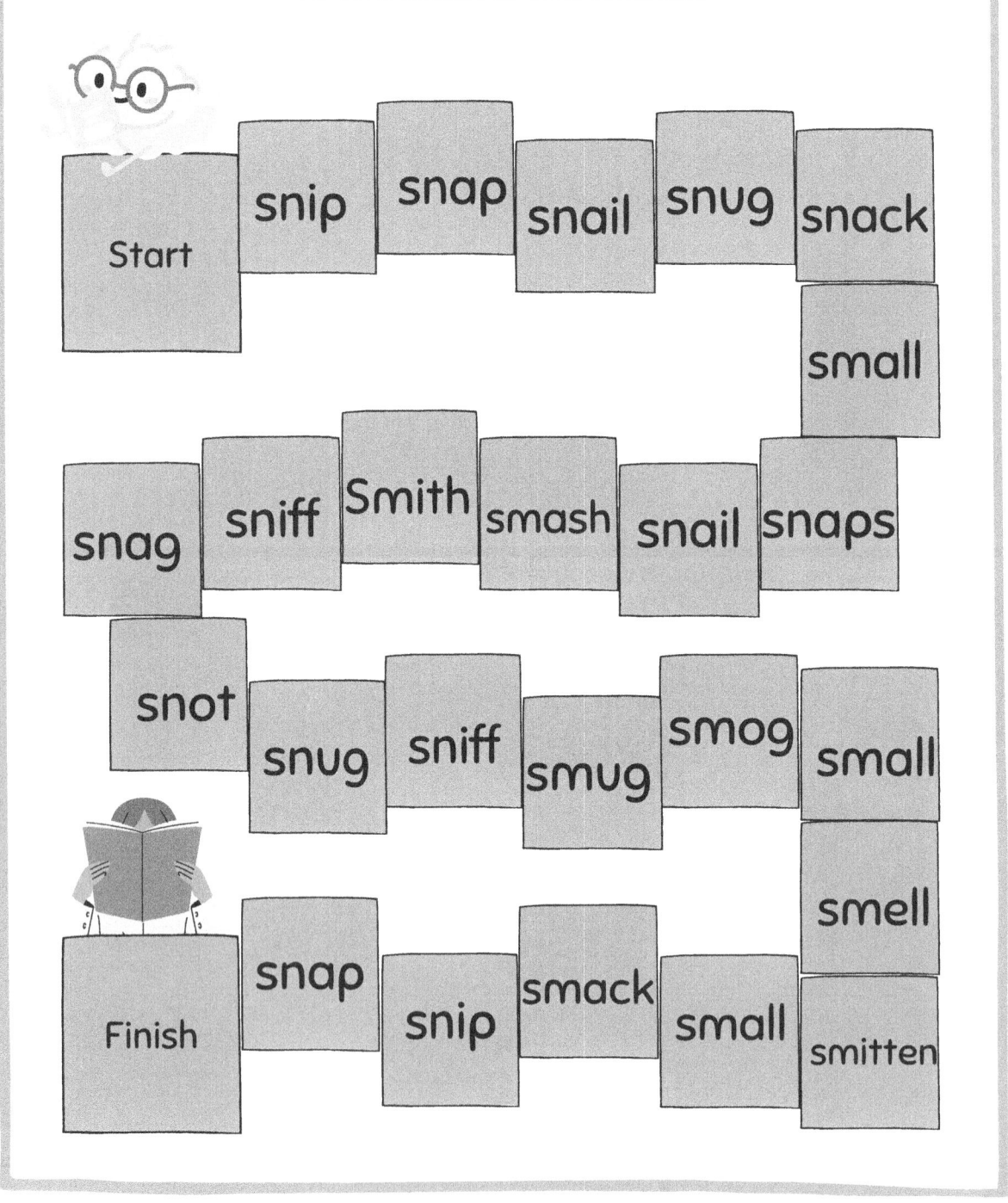

Start → snip → snap → snail → snug → snack → small → snaps → snail → smash → Smith → sniff → snag → snot → snug → sniff → smug → smog → small → smell → smitten → small → smack → snip → snap → Finish

Name: Class:

SET 2
BLEND SN AND SM

Digraph Sn and Sm Sounds

What's that Sound?

Ask your child to isolate the beginning, middle, or final sound in each word. Alternate each day and adjust the lesson to your student's needs. Do not allow them to see the words or the book while doing this exercise.

Snip	Smite
Snake	Smirk
Snort	Smoke

Blending Sounds

Directions: Ask your child to blend the following sounds into words. Do not show them the page.

sn-ar-l   sm-o-g

sn-or-t   sm-ir-k

sn-i-p   sm-i-te

Segmenting Sounds

Directions: Ask your child to break apart the following words into sounds. Do not show them the page.

Snoop   Smack

Snort   Smelt

Snack   Small

Tap it Out

Ask your student to use their finger to tap each circle below each letter of the word as they make it's sound. Then, blend each sound together while they slide their finger over the arrow.

Sn   ai   l

Sn   a   g

Sn   u   g

Tap it Out -2

Ask your student to use their finger to tap each circle below each letter of the word as they make it's sound. Then, blend each sound together while they slide their finger over the arrow.

Sm o g

Sm i r k

Sm a ck s

Read
Read
Read

Directions: Ask the student to read the following sentences.

The smog is soft.

She is smitten.

I see a small snap.

Directions: Ask the student to read the text and color the picture after they are done reading.

The snake slid on the smog. It will sniff and snap at the bugs. Smith sees the snake and stands still. The snake is slim and small. Smith steps back and is snug. Both sit back like snobs.

What's that Word?

Directions: Ask your child to write a letter to create a new word. After they write the letter, read the whole word aloud.

Sma__l   Sn__p

Sn__g   __nap

S__og   Smal__

Card Flip Fun!

Directions: Cut out the cards and place them face down. Take turns flipping the cards over saying the word within five seconds.

Smile	Small
Snake	Snap
Smack	Smitten

First to the Finish

Find a partner. Get a 6 sided die and two make-shift game pieces like a penny or a bead. Take turns rolling the die. Say the word you land on. The first to make it to the finish is the winner.

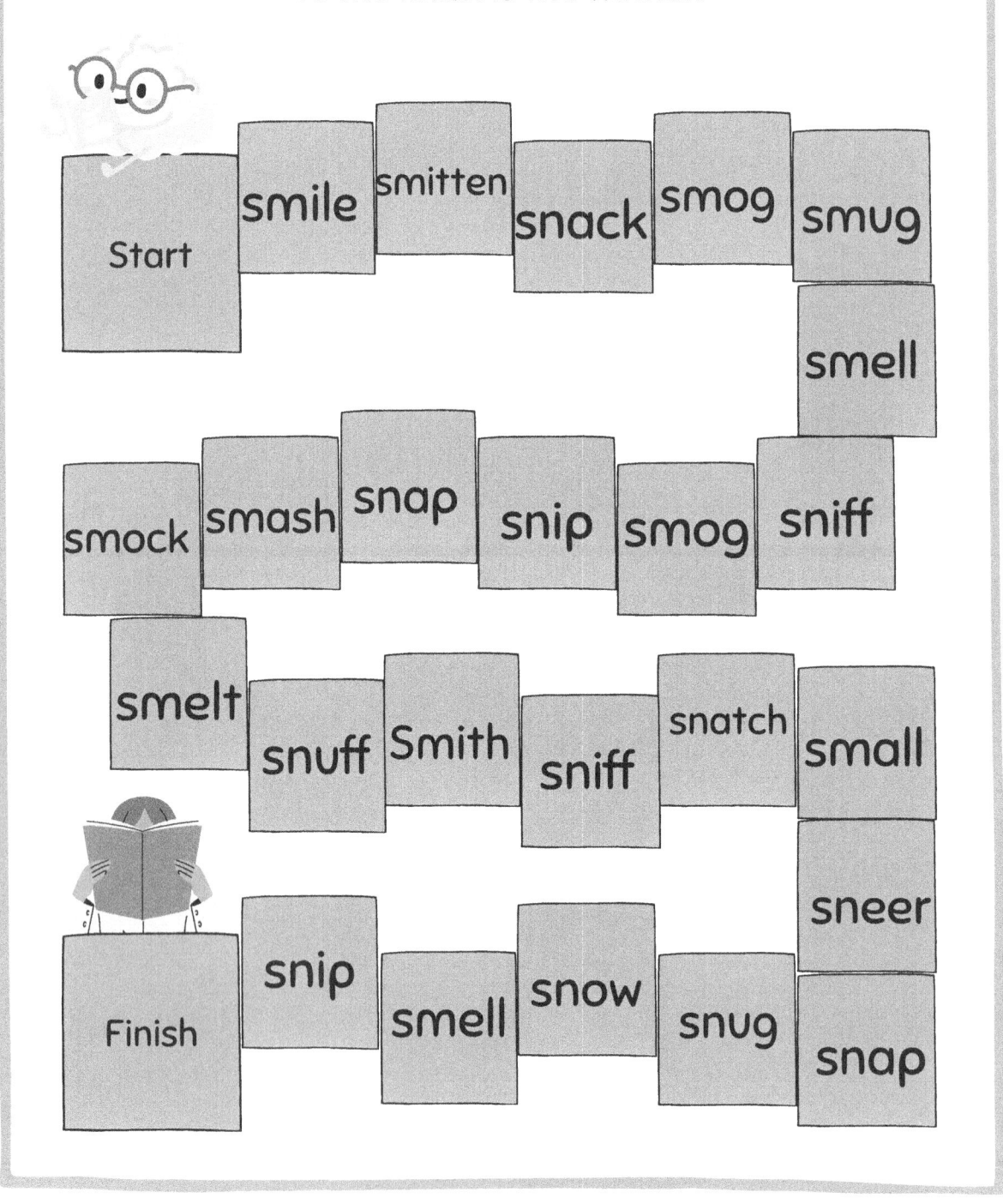

Start → smile → smitten → snack → smog → smug → smell → sniff → smog → snip → snap → smash → smock → smelt → snuff → Smith → sniff → snatch → small → sneer → snap → snug → snow → smell → snip → Finish

Name: Class:

SET 1
BLEND SP AND ST

Digraph Sp and St Sounds

What's that Sound?

Ask your child to isolate the beginning, middle, or final sound in each word. Alternate each day and adjust the lesson to your student's needs. Do not allow them to see the words or the book while doing this exercise.

Spa	Stew
Spy	Stub
Spam	Stand

Blending Sounds

Directions: Ask your child to blend the following sounds into words. Do not show them the page.

Sp-o-t   St-ay

Sp-i-ll   St-ir

Sp-i-n   St-ai-n

Segmenting Sounds

Directions: Ask your child to break apart the following words into sounds. Do not show them the page.

Stick   Spoil

Stain   Speak

Still   Spoon

Tap it Out

Ask your student to use their finger to tap each circle below each letter of the word as they make it's sound. Then, blend each sound together while they slide their finger over the arrow.

Sp i ll s

⟶

Sp u n

⟶

Sp a t

⟶

Tap it Out -2

Ask your student to use their finger to tap each circle below each letter of the word as they make it's sound. Then, blend each sound together while they slide their finger over the arrow.

St a g

St e p s

St i ck s

Read
Read
Read

Directions: Ask the student to read the following sentences.

The stag is big.

Spin the top fast.

The staff can stand still.

Directions: Ask the student to read the text and color the picture after they are done reading.

The stag stands still in the grass. It spots a small bug. The bug spins a web fast. The stag steps back and sniffs. It will go past the big rock. The stag stops and rests. The stag is stands still.

What's that Word?

Directions: Ask your child to write a letter to create a new word. After they write the letter, read the whole word aloud.

Sti_k   St_g

Sp_n   _pin

S_ud   Stu_

Card Flip Fun!

Directions: Cut out the cards and place them face down. Take turns flipping the cards over saying the word within five seconds.

Stick	Spin
Stuff	Span
Stag	Span

First to the Finish

Find a partner. Get a 6 sided die and two make-shift game pieces like a penny or a bead. Take turns rolling the die. Say the word you land on. The first to make it to the finish is the winner.

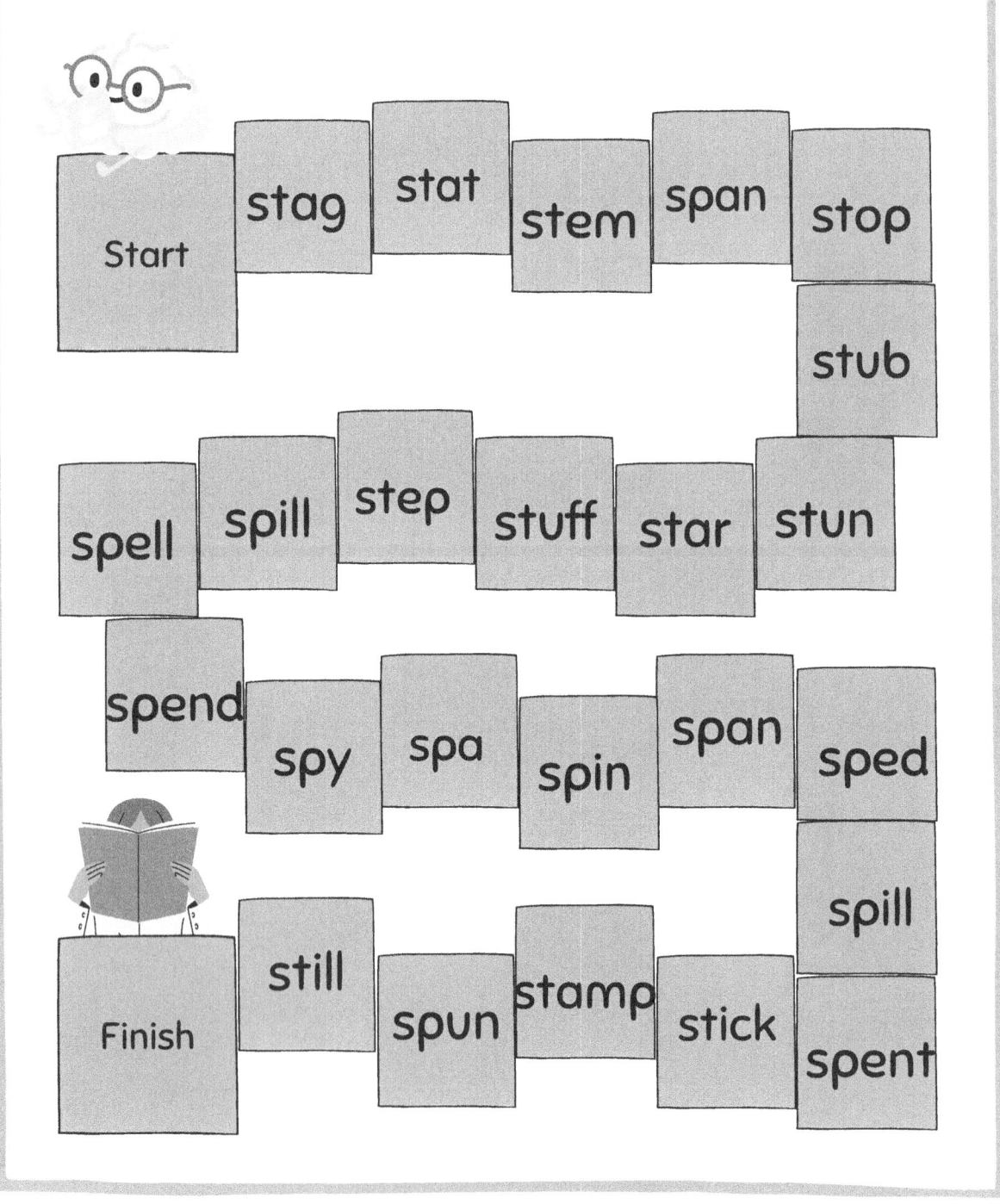

Start → stag → stat → stem → span → stop → stub → stun → star → stuff → step → spill → spell → spend → spy → spa → spin → span → sped → spill → spent → stick → stamp → spun → still → Finish

Name: Class:

SET 2
BLEND SP AND ST

Digraph Sp and St Sounds

What's that Sound?

Ask your child to isolate the beginning, middle, or final sound in each word. Alternate each day and adjust the lesson to your student's needs. Do not allow them to see the words or the book while doing this exercise.

Staff	Space
Stair	Spare
Stale	Spark

Blending Sounds

Directions: Ask your child to blend the following sounds into words. Do not show them the page.

Sp-e-d   St-e-p

Sp-u-n   St-o-p

Sp-i-t   St-u-n

Segmenting Sounds

Directions: Ask your child to break apart the following words into sounds. Do not show them the page.

Stake   Spill

Start   Spoke

Stale   Span

Tap it Out

Ask your student to use their finger to tap each circle below each letter of the word as they make it's sound. Then, blend each sound together while they slide their finger over the arrow.

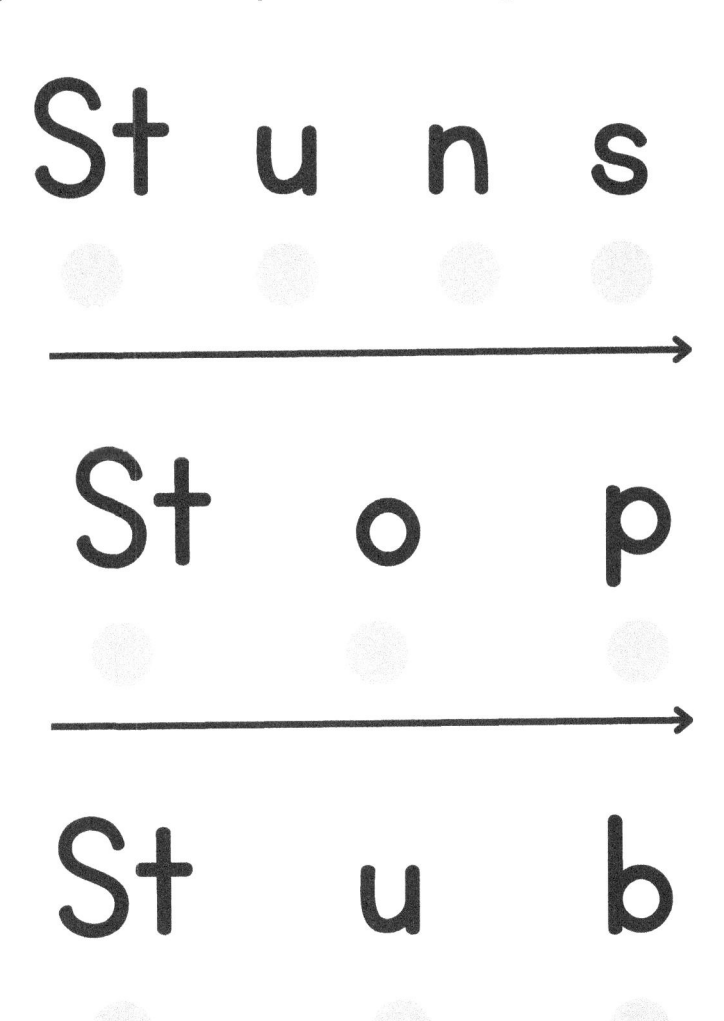

St u n s

St o p

St u b

Tap it Out -2

Ask your student to use their finger to tap each circle below each letter of the word as they make it's sound. Then, blend each sound together while they slide their finger over the arrow.

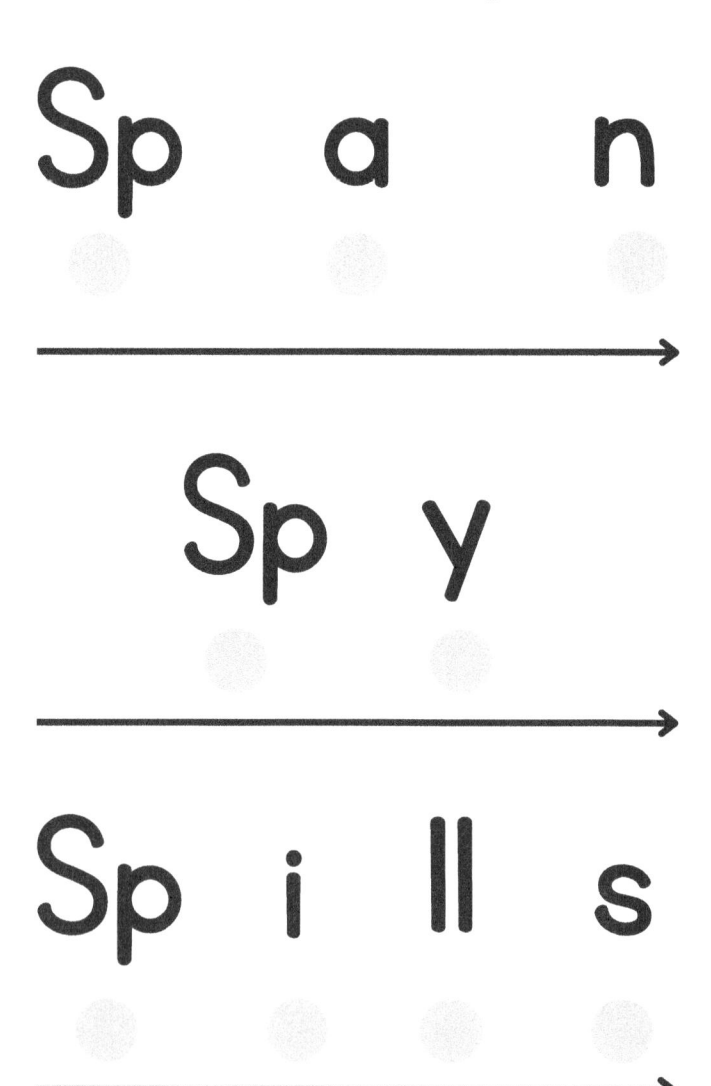

Sp a n

Sp y

Sp i ll s

Read
Read
Read

Directions: Ask the student to read the following sentences.

The stem can stop.

The spy has to stop.

Step on the mat.

Directions: Ask the student to read the text and color the picture after they are done reading.

The spy steps on the spot. He spot is a small bag. The spy spins and stops. He will slip the bag into his vest. The spy must be still and fast. He sprints a long span. The spy did his task!

What's that Word?

Directions: Ask your child to write a letter to create a new word. After they write the letter, read the whole word aloud.

S t a __   S p __ n

S t __ p   __ p i t

S __ u n   S t i l __

Card Flip Fun!

Directions: Cut out the cards and place them face down. Take turns flipping the cards over saying the word within five seconds.

Spill Stand

Spin Stop

Spell Stun

First to the Finish

Find a partner. Get a 6 sided die and two make-shift game pieces like a penny or a bead. Take turns rolling the die. Say the word you land on. The first to make it to the finish is the winner.

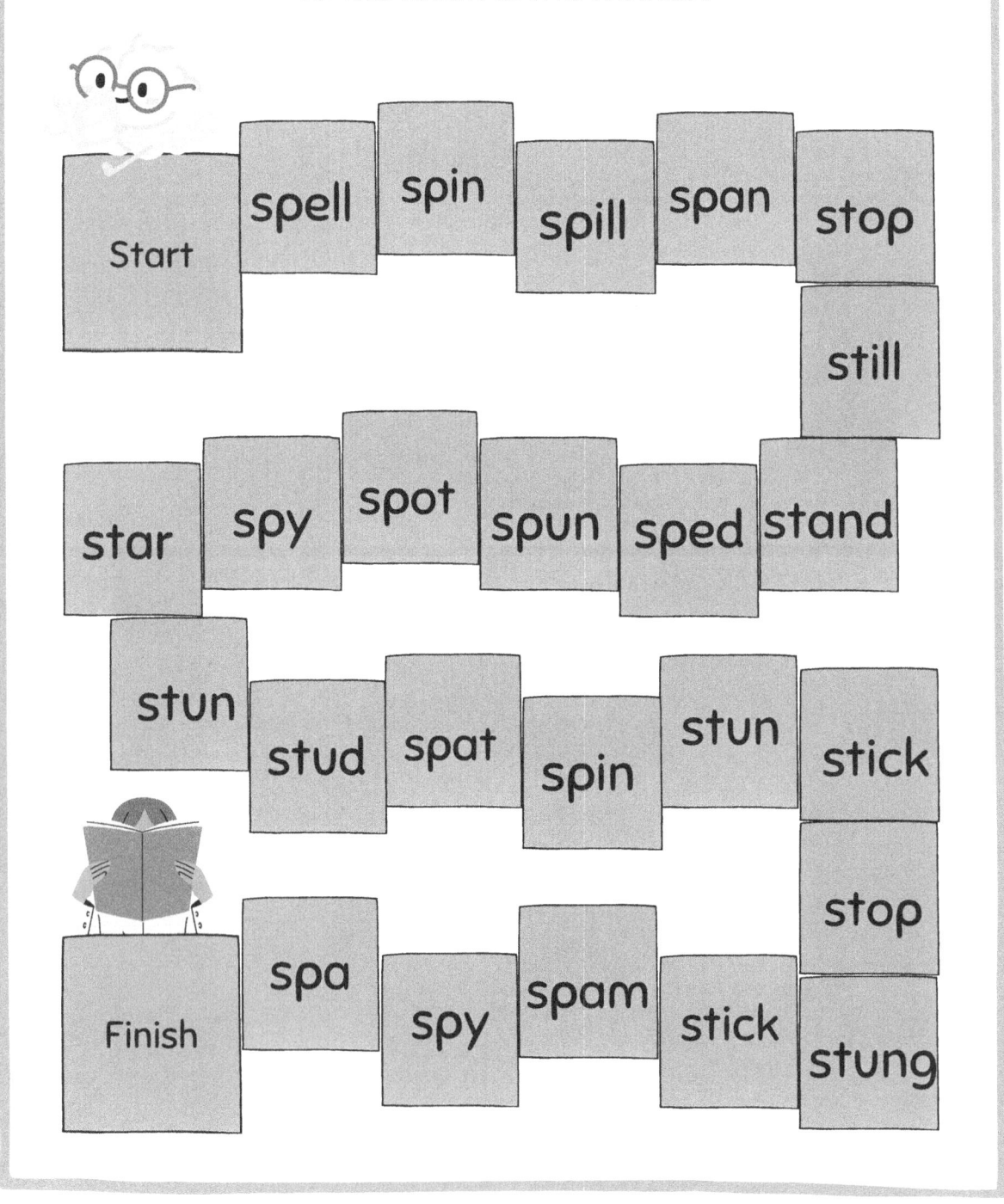

Start → spell → spin → spill → span → stop → still → stand → sped → spun → spot → spy → star → stun → stud → spat → spin → stun → stick → stop → stung → stick → spam → spy → spa → Finish

Name: Class:

SET 3
BLEND SP AND ST

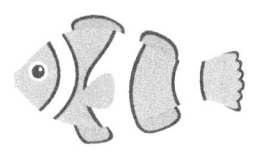

Digraph Sp and St Sounds

What's that Sound?

Ask your child to isolate the beginning, middle, or final sound in each word. Alternate each day and adjust the lesson to your student's needs. Do not allow them to see the words or the book while doing this exercise.

Spade	Stage
Spear	Stark
Spell	State

Blending Sounds

Directions: Ask your child to blend the following sounds into words. Do not show them the page.

Sp-ur   St-e-p

Sp-ar   St-u-d

Sp-y   St-e-m

Segmenting Sounds

Directions: Ask your child to break apart the following words into sounds. Do not show them the page.

Stall   Spare

Stand   Spell

Stead   Spend

Tap it Out

Ask your student to use their finger to tap each circle below each letter of the word as they make it's sound. Then, blend each sound together while they slide their finger over the arrow.

St a ll s

⟶

St u n

⟶

St o p

⟶

Tap it Out -2

Ask your student to use their finger to tap each circle below each letter of the word as they make it's sound. Then, blend each sound together while they slide their finger over the arrow.

Sp a n

Sp i ll s

Sp a m s

Read Read Read

Directions: Ask the student to read the following sentences.

The spot is red.

Stan will stack the cups.

Spin and stop fast.

Directions: Ask the student to read the text and color the picture after they are done reading.

The spider spins a web fast. It spots a small bug. The bug steps on the web and gets stuck. The spider will spin and spin. The bug can not get free. The spider stops to rest. The web is strong and sticky. But the spider has spirit and gets free.

What's that Word?

Directions: Ask your child to write a letter to create a new word. After they write the letter, read the whole word aloud.

S p o __   S p __

S p __ m   __ p a t

S __ a   S p e l __

Card Flip Fun!

Directions: Cut out the cards and place them face down. Take turns flipping the cards over saying the word within five seconds.

Spell	Still
Spend	Stall
Spin	Stuff

First to the Finish

Find a partner. Get a 6 sided die and two make-shift game pieces like a penny or a bead. Take turns rolling the die. Say the word you land on. The first to make it to the finish is the winner.

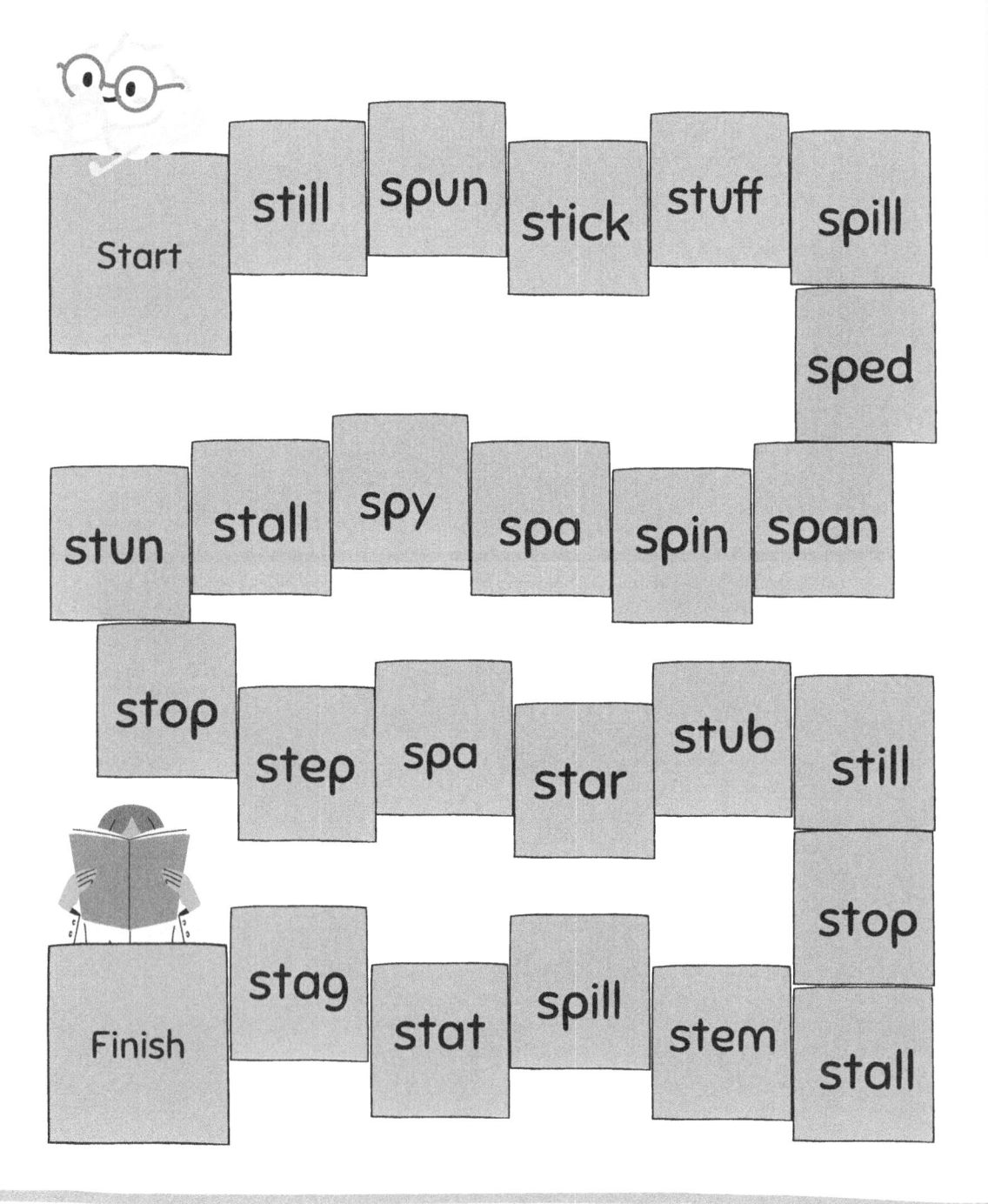

Start → still → spun → stick → stuff → spill → sped → span → spin → spa → spy → stall → stun → stop → step → spa → star → stub → still → stop → stall → stem → spill → stat → stag → Finish

Name: _____ Class: _____

SET 1
BLEND SW AND TW

Digraph Sw and Tw Sounds

What's that Sound?

Ask your child to isolate the beginning, middle, or final sound in each word. Alternate each day and adjust the lesson to your student's needs. Do not allow them to see the words or the book while doing this exercise.

Swim	Two
Swan	Twin
Sweet	Twig

Blending Sounds

Directions: Ask your child to blend the following sounds into words. Do not show them the page.

Tw-o   Sw-e-ll

Sw-i-m   Tw-i-n

Tw-i-g   Sw-a-n

Segmenting Sounds

Directions: Ask your child to break apart the following words into sounds. Do not show them the page.

Sweep   Twine

Swell   Tweet

Swift   Twigs

Tap it Out

Ask your student to use their finger to tap each circle below each letter of the word as they make it's sound. Then, blend each sound together while they slide their finger over the arrow.

Sw e ll

Sw i m

Sw a n

Tap it Out -2

Ask your student to use their finger to tap each circle below each letter of the word as they make it's sound. Then, blend each sound together while they slide their finger over the arrow.

Tw i n

⟶

Tw i g s

⟶

Tw i tch

⟶

Read Read Read

Directions: Ask the student to read the following sentences.

The twig is thin.

She will swim fast.

Twist the top off.

Directions: Ask the student to read the text and color the picture after they are done reading.

The swan swims in the pond. It spots a twig on the water. The swan will twist and dip its neck. A small fish swims by. The swan snaps and misses. The swan swims away and rests. It is still now.

What's that Word?

Directions: Ask your child to write a letter to create a new word. After they write the letter, read the whole word aloud.

Swa__   Sw__m

Tw__g   __wist

T__o   Swel__

Card Flip Fun!

Directions: Cut out the cards and place them face down. Take turns flipping the cards over saying the word within five seconds.

Swim	Swam
Twin	Twig
Swift	Swung

First to the Finish

Find a partner. Get a 6 sided die and two make-shift game pieces like a penny or a bead. Take turns rolling the die. Say the word you land on. The first to make it to the finish is the winner.

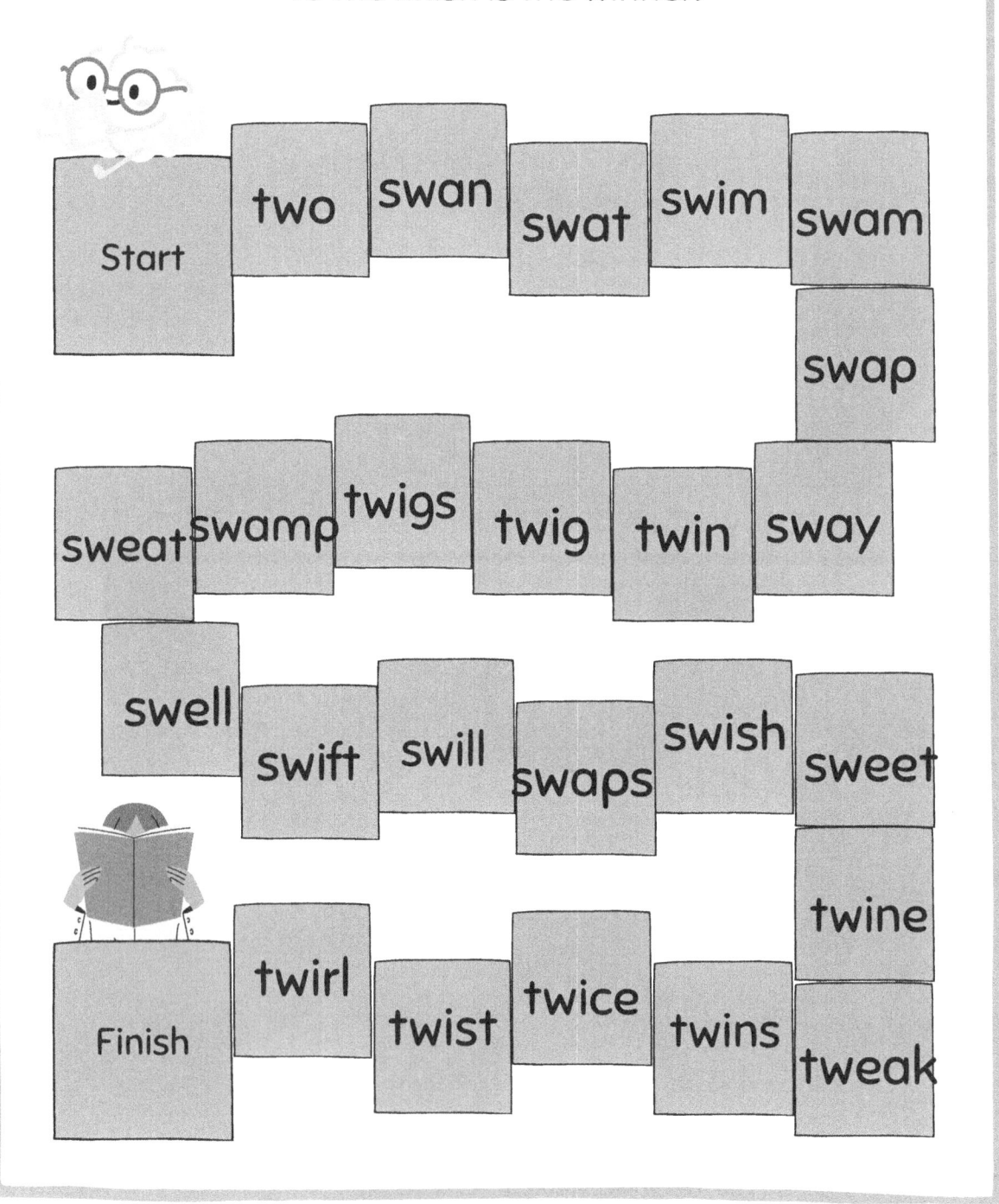

Start → two → swan → swat → swim → swam → swap → sway → twin → twig → twigs → swamp → sweat → swell → swift → swill → swaps → swish → sweet → twine → tweak → twins → twice → twist → twirl → Finish

Name: Class:

SET 2
BLEND SW AND TW

Digraph Sw and Tw Sounds

What's that Sound?

Ask your child to isolate the beginning, middle, or final sound in each word. Alternate each day and adjust the lesson to your student's needs. Do not allow them to see the words or the book while doing this exercise.

Twirl Swarm

Twist Swift

Twice Swipe

Blending Sounds

Directions: Ask your child to blend the following sounds into words. Do not show them the page.

sw-i-m   tw-i-g

sw-e-ll   tw-i-n

sw-i-g   tw-i-n-s

Segmenting Sounds

Directions: Ask your child to break apart the following words into sounds. Do not show them the page.

Sweat   Twice

Sweep   Two

Swish   Tweak

Tap it Out

Ask your student to use their finger to tap each circle below each letter of the word as they make it's sound. Then, blend each sound together while they slide their finger over the arrow.

Sw a p s

Sw a m

Sw i f t

Tap it Out -2

Ask your student to use their finger to tap each circle below each letter of the word as they make it's sound. Then, blend each sound together while they slide their finger over the arrow.

Tw i g

Tw i s t

Tw a n g

Read
Read
Read

Directions: Ask the student to read the following sentences.

The twang is small.

She will swim to the rug.

They are twins.

Directions: Ask the student to read the text and color the picture after they are done reading.

The pig swung in the wet mud. It will twist and swing by the twig. Tim sees the pig swim in the swamp. The pig steps out and sniffs. Tim is swift. The pig trots by the switch. Tim sits by the pig.

What's that Word?

Directions: Ask your child to write a letter to create a new word. After they write the letter, read the whole word aloud.

Twi __   Sw __ p

Sw __ m   __ wat

T __ ist   Swa __

Card Flip Fun!

Directions: Cut out the cards and place them face down. Take turns flipping the cards over saying the word within five seconds.

Swamp   Twist

Swish   Twang

Swell   Switch

First to the Finish

Find a partner. Get a 6 sided die and two make-shift game pieces like a penny or a bead. Take turns rolling the die. Say the word you land on. The first to make it to the finish is the winner.

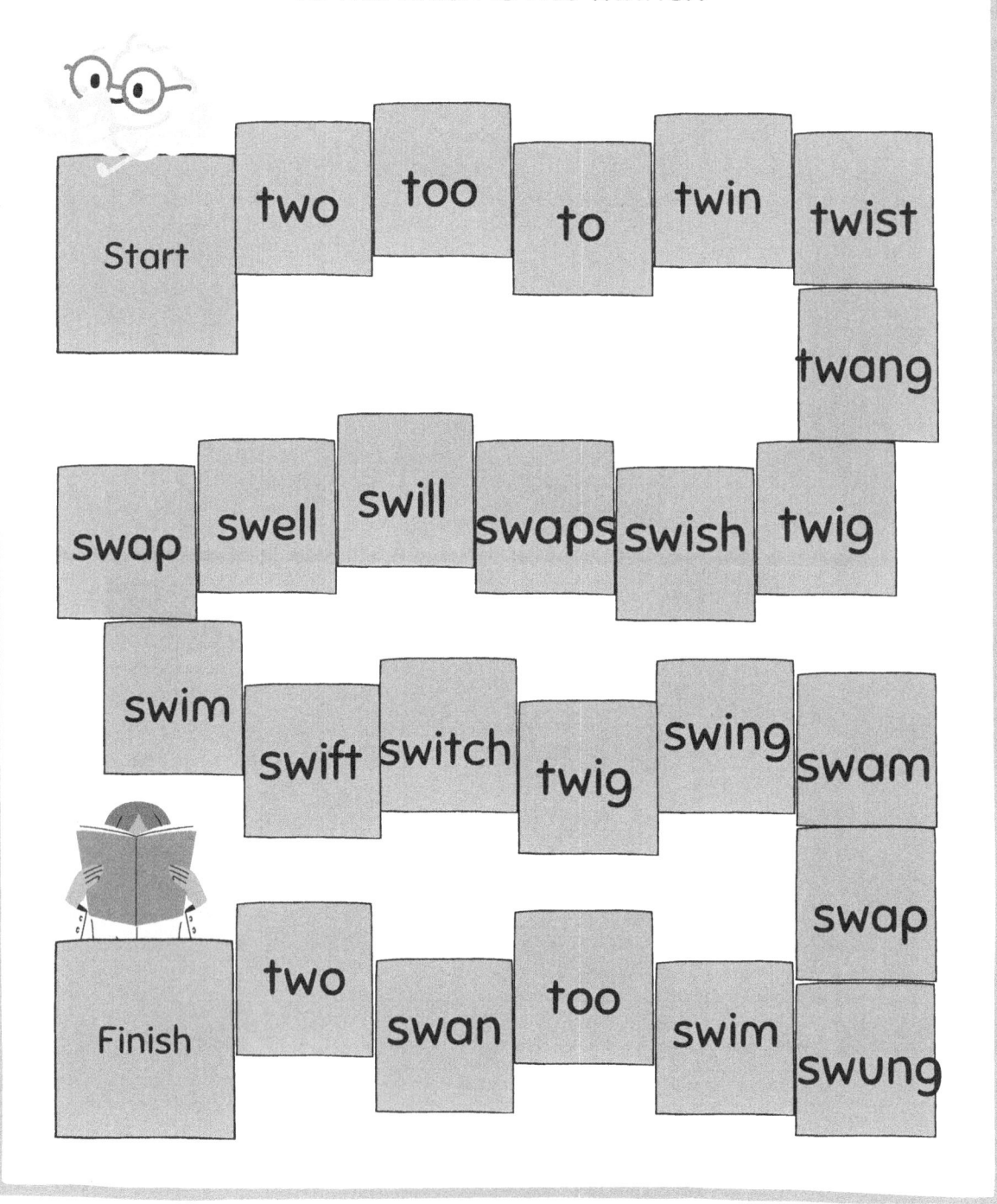

Start → two → too → to → twin → twist → twang → twig → swish → swaps → swill → swell → swap → swim → swift → switch → twig → swing → swam → swap → swung → swim → too → swan → two → Finish

Name:　　　　　　　　　Class:

SET 1
BLEND SCR, THR, SHR

Digraph Scr, Thr, Shr Sounds

What's that Sound?

Ask your child to isolate the beginning, middle, or final sound in each word. Alternate each day and adjust the lesson to your student's needs. Do not allow them to see the words or the book while doing this exercise.

Scram   Throb

Scrub   Shred

Three   Shrub

Blending Sounds

Directions: Ask your child to blend the following sounds into words. Do not show them the page.

shr-u-b   thr-ee

scr-u-b   shr-ew

thr-o-b   scr-a-p

Segmenting Sounds

Directions: Ask your child to break apart the following words into sounds. Do not show them the page.

Shred   Scrap

Shrew   Threw

Screw   Throw

Tap it Out

Ask your student to use their finger to tap each circle below each letter of the word as they make it's sound. Then, blend each sound together while they slide their finger over the arrow.

Sh r e d

Sh r u b

Th r o b

Tap it Out -2

Ask your student to use their finger to tap each circle below each letter of the word as they make it's sound. Then, blend each sound together while they slide their finger over the arrow.

Th r ee

Sc r u b

Sc r a m

Read
Read
Read

Directions: Ask the student to read the following sentences.

The shrimp can swim.

Scrub the pot clean.

The three cats shrug.

Directions: Ask the student to read the text and color the picture after they are done reading.

The king has a shred of cloth to sit on. The shred is thick and did not shrink. He will sit and think. The king will shrug and scratch his chin. The king grins as he thinks of fresh shrimp chips. What a thrill.

What's that Word?

Directions: Ask your child to write a letter to create a new word. After they write the letter, read the whole word aloud.

Thr__ll   Sc__am

Sh__ed   __hred

S__rew   Thro__

Card Flip Fun!

Directions: Cut out the cards and place them face down. Take turns flipping the cards over saying the word within five seconds.

Three   Scrub

Throw   Shrug

Scrap   Shrub

First to the Finish

Find a partner. Get a 6 sided die and two make-shift game pieces like a penny or a bead. Take turns rolling the die. Say the word you land on. The first to make it to the finish is the winner.

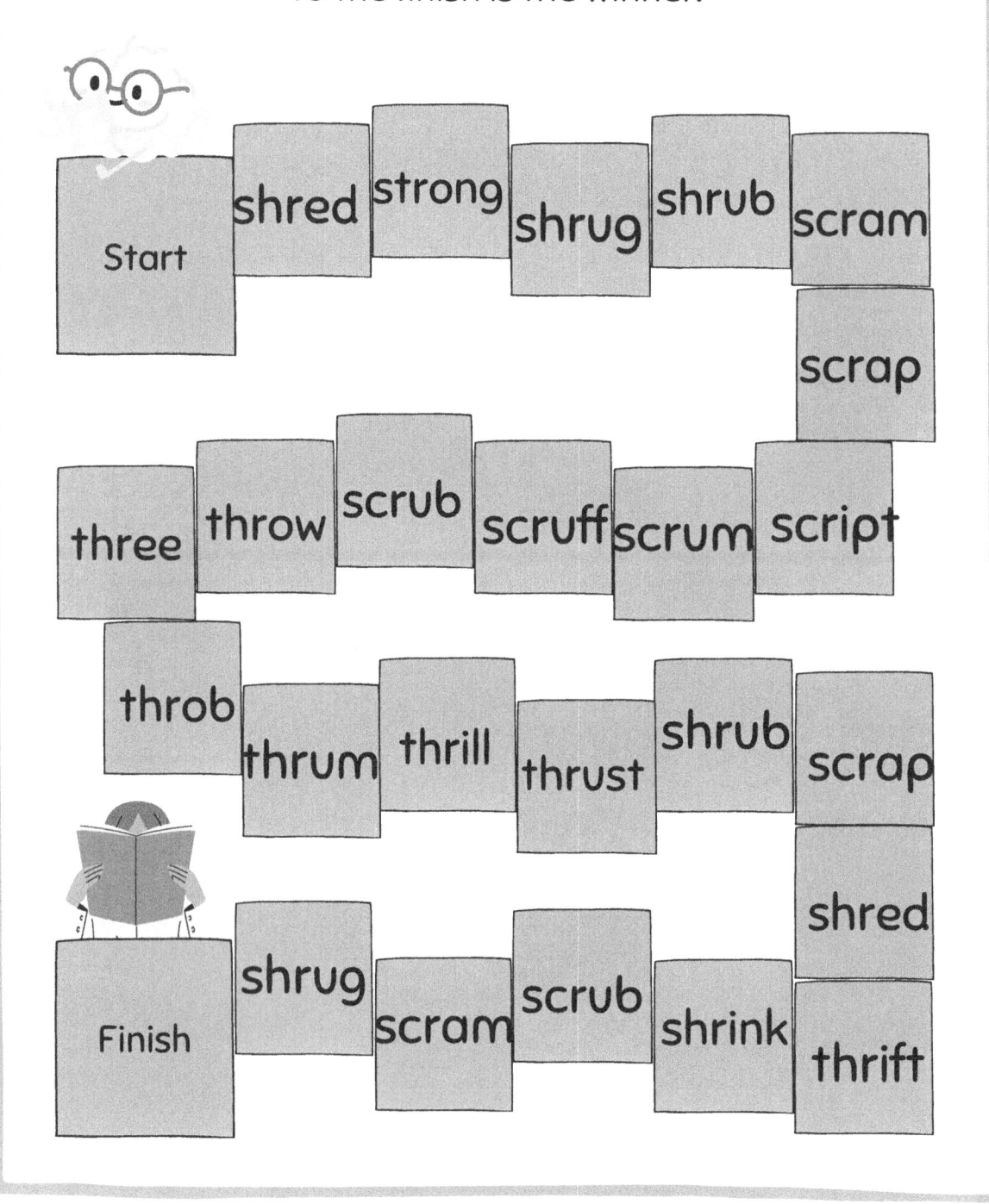

Start → shred → strong → shrug → shrub → scram → scrap → script → scrum → scruff → scrub → throw → three → throb → thrum → thrill → thrust → shrub → scrap → shred → thrift → shrink → scrub → scram → shrug → Finish

Name: Class:

SET 2
BLEND SCR, THR, SHR

Digraph Scr, Thr, Shr Sounds

What's that Sound?

Ask your child to isolate the beginning, middle, or final sound in each word. Alternate each day and adjust the lesson to your student's needs. Do not allow them to see the words or the book while doing this exercise.

Thrust   Three

Scrap   Shrub

Shrink   Shred

Blending Sounds

Directions: Ask your child to blend the following sounds into words. Do not show them the page.

sc-r-e-e   th-r-e-w

sc-r-e-w   sh-r-e-w

th-r-o-w   sh-r-e-d

Segmenting Sounds

Directions: Ask your child to break apart the following words into sounds. Do not show them the page.

Three   Scrum

Threw   Shrub

Scram   Shrug

Tap it Out

Ask your student to use their finger to tap each circle below each letter of the word as they make it's sound. Then, blend each sound together while they slide their finger over the arrow.

Shr u g

Shr i n k

Thr i f t

Tap it Out -2

Ask your student to use their finger to tap each circle below each letter of the word as they make it's sound. Then, blend each sound together while they slide their finger over the arrow.

Thr u s t

⟶

Scr a m

⟶

Scr u n ch

⟶

Read
Read
Read

Directions: Ask the student to read the following sentences.

She will shred the shrub.

The cat will shrink.

Throw the ball fast.

Directions: Ask the student to read the text and color the picture after they are done reading.

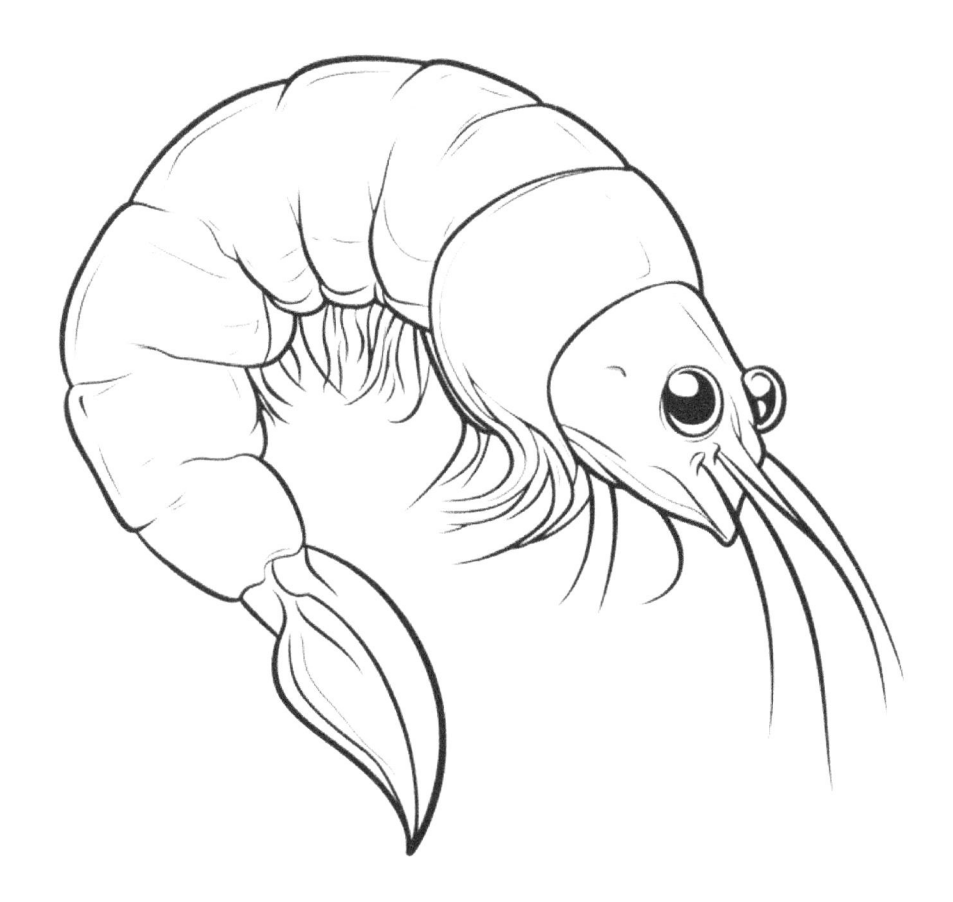

The shrimp swims in a small pond. It will thrust and flip fast. A frog sees the shrimp. The shrimp will shrink back and scratch. The frog jumps and throws a splash. The shrimp scrubs the scrap.

What's that Word?

Directions: Ask your child to write a letter to create a new word. After they write the letter, read the whole word aloud.

Thr__e   Sc__ap

Sh__nk   __hrub

T__rift   Thri__

Card Flip Fun!

Directions: Cut out the cards and place them face down. Take turns flipping the cards over saying the word within five seconds.

Thrill	Scram
Throb	Shred
Scrub	Shrug

First to the Finish

Find a partner. Get a 6 sided die and two make-shift game pieces like a penny or a bead. Take turns rolling the die. Say the word you land on. The first to make it to the finish is the winner.

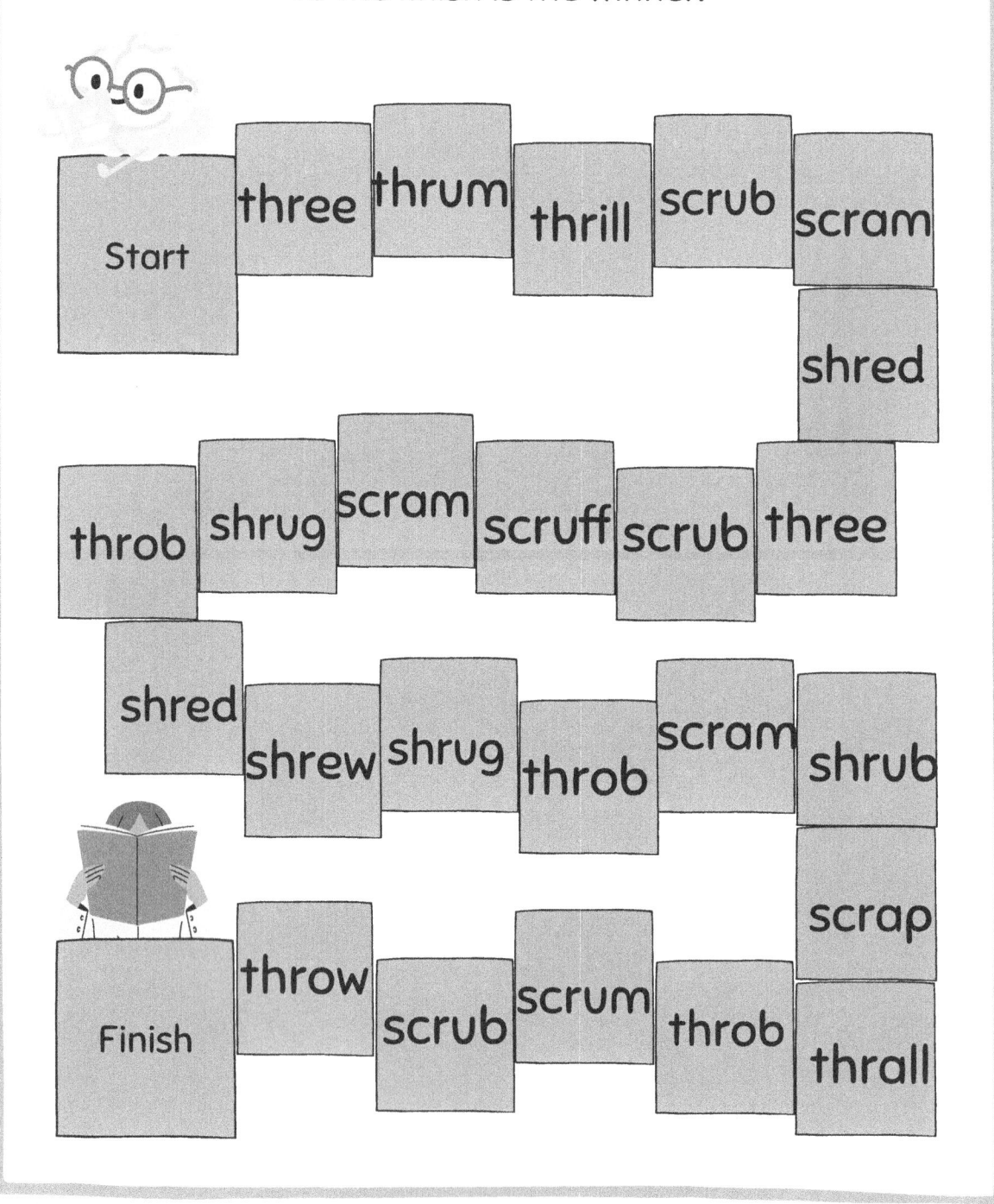

Start → three → thrum → thrill → scrub → scram → shred → three → scrub → scruff → scram → shrug → throb → shred → shrew → shrug → throb → scram → shrub → scrap → thrall → throb → scrum → scrub → throw → Finish

Made in United States
Orlando, FL
04 February 2025